LESSONS FROM THE FRONT LINES

Insights from 40 years
on the battlefield of
small business!

KURT SCHAUERMANN

EDK BOOKS

Published by EDK Books and Distributed by EDK Distribution, LLC
edkbooksanddistribution.com
edkbooksanddistribution@gmail.com | (206) 227-8179

Lessons From The Front Lines

ISBN: 978-1-956065-27-5

Library of Congress Control Number: 2026911727

Printed in the United States of America

Editor: Barbara Kindness
Cover Design-Book Layout: Julie K. Lee @ Lee Creative

Image(s) used in this book's design contain no AI-generated content.

ENDORSEMENTS

"Kurt mentored me from a University of Washington Business student into a multi-unit management role in three years. Four years after that, I became a partner and ultimately bought my own franchise locations. Kurt practiced a deeply personal and ethically principled leadership approach. He is selfless and reflective and was the foundation of my business career."

– **Bret Stewart**, President of a multi-unit franchise system of more than nineteen locations

"Kurt has a treasure chest of leadership knowledge that I had the privilege of getting to tap into from a young age. From 'tough on standards, easy on people' to 'are you running the business or is the business running you?' are not only my two most quoted lines of his, but they were the bedrock of my leadership foundation. I am so thankful for his wisdom and guidance."

– **Steve Bradshaw,** Vice President of Operations for a multi-unit food service system

"Kurt coached me not just on how to manage, but on how to listen. His guidance showed me that respect, empathy, and understanding are the foundation of great leadership. Kurt's mentorship shaped the manager and now owner/operator that I am today."

– **Amanda Riley,** business owner and former employee

"Our law office employed the services of Kurt Schauermann in 2014 as a business consultant. We were facing the sudden and unexpected retirement of one of the firm's two founding partners and we had certain key employees that we did not want to risk losing as part of that transition.

"Kurt's wisdom, experience in HR matters, and business management insights were instrumental in helping us to effectuate the partner's retirement without a hitch.

"Our transition went smoothly and the law firm continued to function and grow due in large part to Kurt's input and sound advice."

– **William K. Thayer,** Attorney and Author

DEDICATION

G.L. "JERRY" SCHAUERMANN

I dedicate this book to my father, G.L. "Jerry" Schauermann (1926-2014), who gave me a chance when I wasn't very mature, wise or valuable. He was at times my boss, my partner, and my lender. Many times, his lessons were hard for me to learn but he was patient and more stubborn than I was. "Things I learned from my Dad" is always near the top of my re-reading list.

TABLE OF CONTENTS

PART 3 – ENGAGEMENT

AUTHOR'S NOTE

Beginning in January of 1980, I started compiling and writing memos to our franchise store managers and in some cases to the entire crews. There was no intention of providing sage wisdom. My purpose was to make sure the culture of our company that had survived challenging times (and would survive more tough times over the next forty years) would endure. Our culture and philosophy were really my dad's mantra, so to speak. He was a salesman. He grew up in the 1930s and '40s on a farm in Colorado, served in World War II, married, and had raised a family. He had strong feelings about right and wrong, fair and unfair, and how you treated customers. Eventually, that philosophy he lived by became the core values of our company. A group of managers and I attempted to codify that philosophy into a Mission Statement and into our manuals and operations guides. We were probably only about 75 percent successful, but we did enjoy some benefits from the process. We had great discussions about what was important to our guests and to our staff members. We did a lot of surveying of our crews. In 2000, I enrolled in the Executive MBA program at the University of Washington Foster School of Business. In that program, my small group did a project using our company as the laboratory. The topic was Change Management, and my classmates did quite a number of interviews with managers and team leaders. The goal was to determine how best to communicate a major change in our company and what we needed to do to preserve the great staff we had. Our management team averaged over sixteen years of tenure. This was very unusual in our segment of the food service industry (Fast Food in Enclosed Malls). If the company was going to survive the anticipated change, we needed to keep those good people! I have divided the memos into "Management" focused and “Leadership” focused. Some are more practical and directed toward specific daily advice (Management). Others deal with longer-term team and culture building (Leadership) advice. Although there is some overlap and common processes in such topics as Listening, I divided them into separate parts and added Engagement as this is an important component in running a sustainable business. I wrote these Manager memos between 1980 and 2016. They often speak very specifically about the food service business but hopefully you can see a connection to your industry, business, or organization. I hope you enjoy it and get some ideas from them. And, I hope something shared here will save you some grief as well as provide some wisdom learned at the “School of Hard Knocks”!

– **Kurt Schauermann**

INTRODUCTION

The following memos and stories are drawn from more than forty-two years of experience operating a small business. S&W/Centerfoods ("Centerfoods") managed up to twenty-four quick-serve food service operations, primarily located in shopping centers, and employed as many as three hundred and sixty team members at one time.

Many of these stories come from over thirty-five years of monthly "Manager Memos" written for store managers and Team Leaders. Others are inspired by advice and insights from successful leaders across a range of industries.

Not all of our "stores," as we call them, were profitable. Anyone who has been in the restaurant business for any length of time—and has operated more than two locations—has likely experienced at least one "loser." Still, we stayed grounded in our guiding theme:

"S&W/Centerfoods is Good People Who Care."

This phrase reflects the caring culture we work hard to cultivate at every level. Our managers care about their people. Our staff members care about their guests. Our leaders care about everyone they interact with—whether vendors, guests, or employees.

Caring begins with listening.

I'll admit I wasn't always a good listener. As a young manager, I was often more interested in being heard than in hearing others. Over time, I've worked to close my mouth and open my ears.

At my father's memorial service, I was deeply moved by the number of people who shared stories about how he had touched their lives—

simply by being a good listener. People joined his church because after a service he would approach them and say, "You look like someone I should know. Tell me about yourself." He had a gift for walking into a room, and within ten minutes he knew more about some people there than many of their close friends knew.

I'm not naturally that way. I'm not as spontaneous as he was. But over the years, I've learned to slow down and make space to understand people—their stories, their motivations, what "floats their boat." I believe everyone can become a better listener. I also believe we are called to be good stewards of what's entrusted to us, including our businesses. Our companies give us the chance to be deeply involved in people's lives and to make a lasting, positive impact. I often meet fellow business owners who share stories of employees who have overcome hardships and have gone on to thrive. What I've learned is this: becoming a better listener and treating others with care and concern yields rewards far beyond business success.

Throughout this book, I use real stories to illustrate both strong outcomes and difficult challenges. My goal is to help prepare others for the stress and anxiety that come with running a business and managing a team.

A Framework for the Book

Part 1, Management, is about directing and coaching tasks—daily, weekly, and monthly.

Here are practical tools to help managers get things done in a workplace that depends on cooperation. Topics include hiring and training, discipline, delegation, time management, and navigating difficult team dynamics.

Part 2, Leadership, is about building a workplace that succeeds over the long term. This means fostering a culture that not only enables management to function but also develops future leaders and long-term employees. Topics include motivation, recognizing high achievers, succession planning, leading through change, and understanding why people stay—or leave.

Part 3, Engagement, is the connection between teams, managers, and leaders. It's the meaningful bond that supports the business, the owners, and—most importantly—the team members.

As a manager, you are continually torn between managing the things inside the store: supplies, equipment, product preparation, and leading people, your Team Leaders and crew members, to achieve high levels of service and successful results. The cruel fact is that throughout the day you must balance where your energy goes. You will also see changes in the demand of your energy as you move into a new season. The high season generally requires much more emphasis on leadership because of more hiring, training, and larger teams of staffs on the floor at any one time. During the post-season period, you have to adjust to the slower times when you are taking care of tasks yourself due to smaller staff and less people on the floor. How do you balance this tension between Things and People? I believe the key is looking at all events as "People-centered". Research indicates that one of the most sought-after benefits in any job is learning. The more you can involve your employees in learning about the tasks and things of the job, the more they will appreciate their job and the easier time you will have in managing the things in the store. I know it's not always practical to teach someone about a piece of equipment or about ordering if you are alone in the store. What about asking them to make out an order in the evening before they go home? What about having a crew person call in the order, so you don't have to? When a Team Leader calls you at home to ask a question, what is the first thing out of your mouth? Do you provide the answer, looking at it as another one of those things you must deal with, even on your day off? Or do you ask the Team Leader "What do you think should be done?" or "What do you want to do?"

Asking the question before providing an answer is what a leader does. A manager of things provides the answer first and never has to lead their crew person or Team Leader to a higher level of achievement.

Managers are forgotten. Leaders are remembered!

PART 1

MANAGEMENT

KURT SCHAUERMANN

YOU KNOW STUFF! NOW LISTEN!

You wouldn't have become a manager or owner if you didn't know a lot! Still, even after reaching a certain level of career success, it's common to feel over your head at times.

That's okay.

You are surrounded by great people, teachers, and staff—who know more than you do about some very important things. **Listen** to them.

In traditional schools, listening to the teacher is key. In today's more collaborative models, listening to your peers is equally important. The same is true in the workplace. Listening to those around you—those with valuable experience and insights—is vital. At the same time, as the owner or manager, your decisions must be heard and executed. That creates a natural tension: between seeking input and bearing responsibility for the outcome. Great management and great leadership require more than just strategy and decision-making. They require **engagement**—a genuine connection with the people you lead.

Earn the Right to be Heard

Our decisions as leaders are only as effective as the execution that follows. And execution depends on the engagement of the team responsible for carrying out the plan. It's a mistake to assume that just because we hold the title of "Owner" or "Manager," our decisions will be flawlessly executed.

Many new owners and managers quickly realize that a title doesn't automatically earn you the respect or buy-in needed for successful execution. To be truly effective—to be *excellent*—you must earn the right to be heard and followed. And one of the most powerful ways to earn that right is through *listening.*

A FRONT LINE TALE

Jared has worked a few jobs in his life. He often ends up in leadership roles—team lead, store manager—but struggles with frustration when his team doesn't match his level of commitment.

While sitting on a dock by a quiet lake outside Cooperstown, New York, I asked Jared who the best boss he ever had was. He answered without hesitation: an area supervisor at Starbucks who had made a lasting impression.

Jared had recently resigned from Starbucks after being promoted to store manager. He'd become disheartened by constant employee turnover and management challenges. But one supervisor stood out. Every time this supervisor visited the store, his first action wasn't to review performance or talk strategy. It was to *check in with Jared.*

He took the time to ask how Jared was doing—personally and professionally—before moving on to his own agenda. His focus was on Jared, not himself. As Stephen Covey wrote in *The 7 Habits of Highly Effective People:* **"Seek first to understand, then to be understood."**

That "others first" approach earned the supervisor credibility, trust, and the opportunity to influence. Jared remembers that supervisor not just as a good leader, but as a life-changing one. That man now owns his own successful business in San Diego, but the leadership lessons he modeled continue to shape the people he once led.

Listening Unlocks Motivation—Knowing Your Team's 'Currency'

We can't truly put others first without being good listeners. And one of the biggest benefits of listening is learning what I call someone's "Currency"—what matters most to them. Their values. Their motivators. The things that energize them and keep them engaged.

Understanding someone's Currency helps you create an environment where they can thrive. It's a lot like parenting: when you know what your child values, you can guide, encourage, and correct them more effectively.

A Call from a Former Employee

One day, my phone rang. The caller ID showed the name of a former manager, Lee. I hadn't heard from her in a while.

"Kurt, hi! It's Lee. I have wonderful news—Mitch and I are getting married!"

I was thrilled for her. Lee had been through a lot. She had two teenage sons from a previous marriage and a younger child from a short-lived relationship. She had managed one of our stores for several years, and I eventually sold her a location in a more rural area near her hometown. Then she said something that stopped me in my tracks:

"I want you to walk me down the aisle and give me away."

I was stunned. I reminded her that she had sons who would be honored to do that, but she insisted:

"You're the closest thing I've ever had to a father."

I cried. It was the highest compliment I've ever received as a business owner.

A FRONT LINE TALE

The Story Behind the Story

When Lee first joined us, she was a seasoned food service professional. She interviewed well and quickly took charge of one of our stores. What we didn't know was that she was two months pregnant and not in a relationship with the baby's father.

She worked hard and had great guest rapport—but there was always some drama. Transportation issues, health concerns, staffing problems—it was constant. After her third son was born, things worsened. She became unreliable—late for shifts, missing days, erratic behavior. It looked like a potential substance issue.

Lee's supervisor and I sat down with her. She denied having a problem but agreed to an assessment. The results confirmed alcohol abuse. We gave her a clear choice: enter an outpatient treatment program or lose her job.

Lee protested—new baby, tight finances, no transportation. We stood firm: no treatment, no job. We made it clear there would be zero tolerance moving forward. Her recovery wasn't perfect. She missed meetings, skipped steps. But she stayed sober and began attending AA. Slowly, but surely, she transformed. The drama faded. Her performance skyrocketed. She became a star.

She needed to move closer to family in Oak Harbor, Washington, and we had a struggling store nearby in Burlington. I told her if she took over, I'd keep it open for at least four more years. She accepted, moved, and turned it around. After two years, I helped her buy the store with an SBA loan.

Though the economy later tanked and she had to close the store, she fulfilled her obligations and moved on with grace. She found community, stayed sober, and built a meaningful life. Today, she's a respected member of her town, active in church and AA, and in a happy marriage.

THE LESSONS:

Where would Lee be if we had just fired her without asking questions? Or worse, ignored her struggles because she was generating profits?

- **Leadership isn't just about driving results. It's about *engagement*. And real engagement starts with listening—*really* listening—to the people who work for you. When you do, they remember. And sometimes, they invite you to walk them down the aisle.**

MANAGEMENT DESCRIBED

Management is a distinct skill set that drives operational excellence and efficiency. Unlike leadership—which often requires patience before results emerge—management efforts can often be measured quickly in day-to-day performance.

A successful manager is attuned to the organization's immediate needs, has a solid understanding of legal and compliance responsibilities, and possesses the practical skills required to execute the core functions of the business. Perhaps most importantly, great managers create an environment where their team operates at a high level—even when they're not present.

Great managers don't just build great teams—they build future leaders.

Tips for Newer Managers/Leaders

Adding Value

My dad often reminded me (when I had recently come to work with him and his partner) that if the job was easy, anyone could do it and he wouldn't need me. It was humbling to hear. That line often carried me through when I was in a tough or demanding situation and thought "Why me?"

I took the same idea and tweaked it a bit. I often shared with newer managers and supervisors that if they were not adding value to their teams, they were not worth the salary I was paying them. I often asked them a simple question: "Did you add value to your team today?" I would encourage all managers to check on if they were "adding Value" regularly.

Without Systems You Have Chaos!

Dad used to tell me that when things seem a mess, when work just seems to be not working, or when I feel up to my eyeballs in snakes, it is time to look at my system (or lack of a system!) to clear out the clutter and the chaos. One thing that has worked well for me, again from my dad, is to take out a pad of paper and just start writing down everything that comes to mind that I need to do, deal with, or that is causing me stress. He told me not to worry about prioritizing things yet. Just get them down on paper. A couple of things often happen. First, the list is never as big on paper as it is when it is just swimming around in your head. Secondly, some things become clear—like you may be stressing on something that is out of your control or someone else's responsibility.

Managing for Excellence

"An excellent job gets done only when the person doing it knows what 'great' looks like."

One of the most common frustrations I hear in the restaurant business field I know well is about poor guest service. Managers and owners often complain that their staff "just doesn't get it." But when I ask them to explain what "it" is, they often struggle to define it clearly.

This is a key problem. We expect people to deliver great service, but we have not clearly defined what that looks like. The saying "Common sense isn't so common" really applies here. In most cases, people want to do a good—even great—job. But they need a picture of what great actually is.

Here is one practical way to bridge the gap: Ask your team what they expect when they go into a restaurant—or any customer-facing business. Write down their answers. This not only gives you an insight into their standards and experiences, but it also engages them in a meaningful dialogue about your expectations.

Defining and Communicating Excellence

Before asking your team for input, it is essential that you and your leadership team clearly define what excellence looks like in your business. What should a guest or customer consistently experience? Whether your business serves people face-to-face, over the phone, or online, this clarity matters.

In our organization, we tackled this by implementing a "Shopper's Survey" program. The process forced us to develop objective, yes-or-no standards for service. It pushed us to define excellence so clearly that we could train to it—and measure it.

We introduced this concept on Day One of the employee orientation. From the beginning, we wanted our team to know that delivering an outstanding guest experience was not just a hope—it was an expectation. When people know what "great" looks like, and that it will be measured, it becomes part of their professional DNA.

The Power of Clarity

I once had an employee who struggled to get to work on time. I coached him. I warned him. I wrote him up. Nothing worked. Finally, during a conversation where I truly listened, he told me, "I'm just not into time, man."

He was a product of his generation, the laid-back ethos of the 1960s—and his values didn't align with the standards of the job. The lesson? **Listening helps you understand people, but it does not mean lowering your expectations.**

Clarity about what is important—like punctuality—is non-negotiable. If someone cannot meet those standards, they may need to work elsewhere. Ironically, most people respect you more when you are clear about your expectations. Listening well means understanding their point of view, even if it does not align with the values of your organization.

Balancing Toughness and Compassion

There is a tension between being a "Servant Leader," as Ron Shaich (founder of Panera Bread) describes, and being a decisive, critical-thinking leader. New managers often fall into one of two extremes:

1. The authoritarian: "My way or the highway."
2. The people-pleaser: "If I just create a positive atmosphere, everything will work itself out."

Both approaches are flawed. Great management requires engagement, listening, and—most critical, clarity. This book's purpose is to help new managers navigate that tension and find a more effective path.

THE LESSONS:

- **Clearly define what excellence looks like for every role.**
- **Do not assume your team shares your vision of great performance. And remember—listening and empathy do not require you to compromise your standards.**
- **Clarity builds confidence. Consistency builds trust. Together, they build great teams.**

Questions to Ponder

What things related to customer service need to be described more completely & specifically?

What can you do to be a better listener of your subordinates? Who can you identify that knows what your customers really want?

What gets in the way of your listening to your people?

NOTES

(Your Own Observations)

ATTITUDE, CHARACTER, MOMENTS OF TRUTH

Perhaps the most critical characteristic of a wonderful manager is their attitude, both toward the work and job and toward their team and customers.

How to Get a Positive Attitude

Years ago, my father gave me one of the greatest gifts I have ever received. He taught me to adopt a POSITIVE ATTITUDE! He also taught me what it *took to develop a positive attitude*—**practice.** That's right, **practice!** How do you practice an attitude? You **start using the words that reflect that attitude,** even when you don't feel that way. When someone asks me, "How are you today?" I try to answer with words that reflect a positive attitude. I will answer "Great!" or "Really good!" with enthusiasm. If I use the terms that reflect a less-than-positive attitude, words like "I'm okay" or "Fine," I start to be less than positive. I challenge each of you to develop a positive attitude by building your vocabulary around positive phrases, not negative or even neutral ones.

Think about what it's like to work around people with **positive attitudes.** Think about what it's like to work around people with neutral or negative attitudes. More importantly, what's it like to date or be married to someone with a positive attitude versus a negative one? It is amazing how people react to you when they detect that positive attitude. ***It's infectious.*** Some of our coworkers and friends are waiting to **reflect the attitude they see** in us. One thing you'll learn in your job as manager is that people take a cue from us. Our attitudes really impact the environment for everyone around us.

Don't get me wrong. There are occasions where it is impossible to reflect a positive approach to real disasters. The reality is that we rarely have those kinds of disasters around us. When someone is dying or seriously ill, when someone's home has burned or been robbed, or when we undergo difficult circumstances of any type, I wouldn't expect you to be "Pollyanna-ish" about it. I do believe that adopting more positive attitudes and practicing them will carry us through those challenging times in our lives.

A FRONT LINE TALE

Jerry was the kind of guy you love to hate. He was always in a good mood and always had something positive to say. When someone would ask him how he was doing, he would reply, "If I were any better, I would be twins."

He was a unique manager because he had several waiters who had followed him around from restaurant to restaurant. The reason the waiters followed Jerry was because of his attitude. He was a natural motivator. If an employee was having a bad day, Jerry was there, telling the employee how to look on the positive side of the situation.

Seeing his style really made me curious, so one day I went up to Jerry and asked him, "I don't get it! You can't be a positive person all the time. How do you do it?"

Jerry replied, "Each morning, I wake up and say to myself, you have two choices today. You can choose to be in a good mood or in a bad mood. I choose to be in a good mood. Each time something bad happens, I can choose to be a victim or I can choose to learn from it. Life is all about choices. When you cut away all the junk, every situation is a choice. You choose how you react in situations. You choose how people will affect your mood. You choose to be in a good mood or a bad mood. The bottom line: It's your choice how you live your life."

What Characteristics Do You Display When the "Pressure Is On"?

I became aware of two incidents that took place in two of our stores. Both involved guests' being very disappointed in our service. The facts of the cases were less important than our response to difficult customers. In both cases, our team members felt "attacked" and challenged to their core. I had just written the month before about our great teamwork and teams in our stores. It was inevitable that despite all our good intentions, we would have guests who are disappointed or even rude to us. This is kind of a "mini crisis" at the counter. **How do you (and your team) respond when the pressure is on?**

Usually, when we have these things happen, after the guest is gone and we have a chance to cool off, we think of all sorts of ways we could/should have responded. By then it is too late, but we vow to do better the next time. **The key question is, how do we do better?** How do we improve our response to crisis and to difficult situations?

Oswald Chambers, a Christian missionary, says we need to practice daily our disciplines for them to show up when the pressure is on. He says it is practice and study in the quiet times BEFORE there is a crisis that will develop our character. If we want our character to be exemplary when that mad guest is standing right in front of us, we need to practice good character traits at all other times. If we believe Courtesy, Confidence, and Kindness are the traits we should display when a guest is rude or unreasonable, we should be practicing them at other times. That may be to our spouse, children, coworkers, parents, and friends.

If you want to always be a person of good character, START NOW! Be the person God desires you to be now. Practice the good characteristics now. Talk to your team about what good character would look like now, before the crisis hits, before the guest is rude to us, before we must acknowledge a mistake and fix it. **Practice it now. Talk about it now. Do role playing to make the practice more practical. Do it now!**

THE LESSONS:

- **Choose to have a positive attitude.**
- **Choose to NOT BE A VICTIM!**
- **Reflect positivity as one of your key characteristics. Practice may not make perfect, but it makes things much better!**
- **Practice the characteristics of being Cool, Calm, and Prepared.**

Questions to Ponder

What can you start practicing to embrace a "Positive Attitude"?

Who in your organization is impacted by your Attitude?

How can you coach others in your organization to reflect a more positive attitude?

NOTES

(Your Own Observations)

Hiring the Best People Starts with CHARACTER

At one point, I had a conversation with a guy who owned a successful small construction company. Lately, he had been feeling overwhelmed—juggling multiple crews, constantly running between job sites, and barely able to catch his breath. He asked how our company managed up to twenty-three separate locations without driving the owner (me) crazy.

That conversation helped me articulate something it took twenty years to fully understand: the most important trait of the people on our **"Good People Who Care"** team was **character.**

Does having good character mean someone is perfect? **Absolutely not.**

Does it mean they never make professional or personal mistakes? **Of course not.**

What it *does* mean is that when mistakes happen, people with character take **responsibility, make amends,** and **learn from them.** It is the willingness to honestly assess one's own weaknesses and not hide or deny them. People of character act with integrity—even when it is inconvenient.

Good character builds **trust**—and trust is the foundation of great management. When I trust someone's character, I do not need to micromanage them. I know they will do the right thing, even when I'm not looking. On the other side, when someone consistently shows a lack of integrity, it erodes trust and slows everything down. You end up spending more time watching them than leading the team.

Why Character Matters

One of the most rewarding things about having people of strong character on your team is the **mutual trust** that develops. Being trusted feels good, builds confidence, strengthens competence, and fosters growth. Leaders can delegate more effectively, and team members rise to higher levels of performance.

But when even one person on the team lacks character, it handicaps the whole group. You are stuck in constant supervision mode. The energy that should go toward growing the business gets diverted to damage control. That is why strong leaders must actively **seek out high-character individuals—and coach up or coach out** those who don't meet that standard.

Hiring for Character: What to Look For

So how do you identify character in an applicant? The interview process can reveal a lot—if you ask the right questions.

Try questions like:

- "Who was your best boss, and why?"

- "Who was your worst boss, and why?"
- "What did you like or dislike about your last job?"
- "What kinds of theft or giveaways did you witness in your last job?"
- "How will you handle it *when* a friend asks you to 'hook them up' with free product?"

These questions aren't about catching someone off-guard. They are about assessing the candidate's **values, self-awareness, and sensitivity to character traits in others.** If someone cannot articulate what made a former leader trustworthy—or doesn't recognize low-character behavior when they've seen it—they may not have developed strong character awareness yet.

That does not mean they're beyond help, but it *does* mean you'll need to spend more time communicating and reinforcing your organization's values and expectations.

The High Cost of Low Character

When low character is tolerated, the consequences ripple across the business. You will often see:

- Increased cash shortages
- Poor guest service
- Workplace conversations dominated by drama, gossip, or distractions
- Decline in team morale and standards

Left unchecked, these cultural cracks can destroy a business from the inside out.

An old survey found that:

- **30% of people won't steal, no matter what.**
- **60% will steal if they believe it is accepted or unlikely to be punished.**
- **10% are actively looking for ways to steal.**

As a manager or owner, your job is to **eliminate that 10% quickly** and create a culture so strong that the 60% wouldn't dream of slipping. When the group norm is rooted in integrity, most people will rise to that standard.

"Reputation is what men and women think of us; character is what God and angels know of us."

– Thomas Paine, patriot

THE LESSONS:

- **Character is the foundation of a successful team—for both managers and team members.**
- **Talent without character is a liability, not an asset.**

Questions to Ponder

How does your organization communicate high character behavior?

Where might you have a blind spot regarding your own character?

Do you have low character individuals you need to filter out of your organization?

NOTES

(Your Own Observations)

Moments of Truth (MOT)

The perception of the guest or customer or employee is formed in their mind by what they observe and sense. There are clearly defined points in time where the guest in your home, the customer at your counter, and the employee in your back room make key observations that form their perceptions. These points in time can also be called "Moments of Truth."

It is in these brief seconds that the guests decide if they are truly welcome in your home and you are glad they are there. It is in this moment that the customer decides if this is an unusual and extraordinary place to spend their money or if they will only get a "standard" experience. It is also in this moment that an employee may decide if this is a place he or she wants to work, give his/her loyalty, and trust the employer.

Just what are these "Moments of Truth" (MOT)? For the guests in your home, the offering of a beverage, a comfortable place to sit, and the willingness to help with a coat are part of the MOT. In full-service restaurants, it has been known for some time that a visit to the restroom is a MOT. If it is clean and sparkling, the perception is that the restaurant is above average in quality and service. For a guest at a quick-service restaurant, the greeting received, be it routine and robotic or warm and sincere, will be a MOT. For employees, the greeting and preparation for the first day of orientation and training is a MOT.

In businesses that are service-oriented and do the majority of their business on the phone or the web, just making a call to customer service can open your eyes to either the excellence you are delivering or...the source of much frustration for your clients and guests.

How are you and your staff doing in your moments of truth for customers? How are you and your shift leaders doing in the MOT for your employees? I am often asked how to motivate employees. My first response is that you do not motivate employees. All you can do is remove obstacles to motivation your employees may have. If we are dealing well with the moments of truth for our employees, it will go a long way toward creating an atmosphere of motivation.

"Clean the corners and the big stuff will take care of itself!"

This is something my very first manager taught me. I occasionally forget it, but it is so true. Look around your business. Look in the corners, under counters and tables, behind machines and down in the dark recesses where you have not looked recently. Look at your personal grooming and personal space. I think you will be a little embarrassed at what you will see. It is not unusual to get a little lax in deep cleaning when we are in the everyday activities, but…it is time to dig deep and clean the nooks and crannies of your store.

What does the kick plate on the swinging door look like? Have you run your hands over the edges of the door, the counter out front, or other places your guests touch but you do not have occasion to? If you take care of these spaces (and get your crew members to participate!), big stuff will seem so obvious that it will require little encouragement to get it clean.

Have a contest by putting something in a corner or deep cleaning area and giving a reward to the employee who finds it and cleans it in that area. Function as inspectors for each other so that you hold each other accountable for clean, not just "good enough".

All of this makes perfect sense in a restaurant setting but think about any business. Whether you are in outside sales, other retail environments, or doing business on the internet, the environment you create visually sends important clues to your staff and to your customers about your professionalism and how serious you take your business *and* their business.

Serving on the advisory council for a franchise organization, a lesson was learned by the franchise leadership in the middle of a meeting. The executives were discussing the need for franchise operators to report issues with products coming into the location using an 800 number. The problem was that once you called the number you were directed to a long phone tree that really discouraged operators from diving into it. The result was products that were not suitable for resale weren't being fixed or replaced. We challenged the executives to call the number during the meeting. The first-hand experience of seeing what operators had to deal with caused a seismic shift in the discussion. The operators were the customers of the franchise organization. The franchise executives realized that what they understood to be happening just wasn't. The MOT for the operators was the ease of dealing with the franchise organization.

THE LESSONS:

- **Identify the Moments of Truth in your business. Ask customers and team members what they consider important Moments of Truth. Then deliver them!**
- **Look closely at things you may often take for granted. See things through your teammates' and customers' eyes. Fix the little things and the important things may start to take care of themselves.**

Questions to Ponder

Have you tried lately to have a customer experience in your business? If you operate with a website, have you logged on as a customer to see how easy it is to navigate? If you do business on the phone, have you called your 800 number lately as a customer to see how long the telephone tree is and how easy (or difficult!) it is to navigate?

What are the MOTs for your business?

What is the first contact your customers have with your business? The first "touch point"?

What messages are you sending to your customers or potential customers about your business?

NOTES

(Your Own Observations)

EMPLOYEE RETENTION: HOW TO ATTRACT AND KEEP THE BEST

A Key to Hanging On to the Best People—Your Attitude

As a first-line manager, you are the ones who reflect either a cheerful outlook about our industry and the daily work or reflect a negative one. If you want to attract the best people, you must reflect the best attitude about your workplace. The number one thing people cite as the most positive part of their job is their coworkers and boss. People want to work in a place that is positive and where people reflect positive attitudes toward themselves and each other.

You are *all* customers. Can you tell the atmosphere of a retail/store/restaurant by the attitudes of the crew members you first contacted? Of course you can. When it is negative, what do you assume about that boss? When it is positive, what do you assume about that boss? When you interview people, a key question is, "Tell me about the best boss you ever worked for. What made them a great boss?" How would your staff/team members answer that question about you? If that is a question asked at the interview, it is one you should be asking about yourself as you go about your workday. Do you ever ask your team how you can improve? What do they tell you? When I ask you what they think of you, will you know?

Another thing that will improve the atmosphere and the retention in your store is the way you view your own job. A suggestion I got from a particularly good counselor several years ago was to be sure to share with your family (spouse, partner, kids, friends) the good parts of your day. We all usually vent when we come home after work. We readily share the negative parts of our day. It is no wonder why kids grow up thinking of work as a thing to avoid. If you will consciously work at sharing the good parts of your workday—an employee who was successful, a guest who expressed appreciation for your extra effort, another store manager who complimented you on your crew, or any other positive event—two things will happen.

First, you will start to be more conscious of the positive parts of your work; and second, your friends, kids, and spouse or partner will start to be more positive about work and, in particular, *your* work. They will be your supporter instead of another person you have to "do battle with." The greatest gift you can give your kids is a positive attitude toward work. It is never too late!

Are You Bringing Out the Best in Your People?

Here is a challenge to all managers and shift supervisors: Each week pick one or two people who you are going to train and develop to a higher level of performance, WITH INTENTION!

What do I mean "With Intention"? My experience is that people thrive and are encouraged when a boss takes time to lay out a plan for their development. It does not have to be a huge "management" training program. What I am referring to is figuring out what talents and natural abilities one or more of your people have and then identifying how you can apply that talent to a need of your store. Perhaps a person is artistic. Perhaps there is a mechanically inclined person on your staff. Maybe you have a person who is a "perfectionist" when it comes to orderliness and cleanliness. I cannot think of a business that would not benefit from all of these skills, if applied with intention and with some explanation as to what needs to be accomplished.

We had a store manager many years ago who recognized he was a bit weak in keeping the store clean and maintained. He had an extraordinary young woman who was a classic "Neatnik". She became the "Backroom Monitor." It was her job to set standards for cleanliness and to hold everyone accountable to that standard, including the manager! She took immense pride in the improvement made to that store. The manager was relieved to have an area in which he was weak become excellent whenever his boss came into the unit. The crew adopted the "Backroom Monitor" as another leader in the store. It was a classic "win-win-win" situation.

We have had other managers identify people who were interested in and particularly good at putting up marketing materials and merchandising the store. They handed off the duties of preparing for a new promotion and monitoring the condition of the merchandising to those special people. They had to coach them on the expectations of the company and the goal of the promotions. They had to set a schedule so they could be there to set up, take down, and store the materials. They had to provide feedback and encourage the people but, overall, the job was done more effectively and the morale of the crew persons was enhanced.

Where can you build up your team by delegating and coaching one or more members of your crew? Now is the time!

THE LESSONS:

- **Check your attitude toward work. Share the good parts of your work with both loved ones and your team. Be the boss your team members will talk about at their next interview, in a positive light.**
- **Identify talents in your current team and make use of them. Delegate work to enhance their satisfaction and ease your long-term demands.**

- **As the economy improves, we struggle like many to find great staff persons. Sometimes the best ones are right under our nose if we just open our eyes and our ears.**

Questions to Ponder

How do you prepare to walk into your business and put your positive, best foot forward?

How do you prepare to walk in the door at your home? Do you share the good after venting the bad?

How often do you ask your team what they want in their job? Do you know what their "currency" is?

What are three things you can do to enhance the learning and experience of your good people?

NOTES

(Your Own Observations)

THE GEMS RIGHT UNDER OUR NOSE

A FRONT LINE TALE

I heard about Amanda from Matt, our manager at the Tacoma, Washington, store over the course of a few months. She had been working part time for us and had at least one other job, and at times two other jobs. She was a senior in high school and other than that I only knew that our manager said she was a terrific employee, but he couldn't get her to quit her other jobs. She needed the money. Matt warned me that she had some "unorthodox looks". He didn't elaborate so I arranged to come by the store when she was scheduled to work so I could meet her and see if we could offer her more than a part-time position.

When I came into the back room, Matt introduced me to Amanda. I was taken aback at first glance. She had some obvious tattoos and a few piercings in places other than her ears. She also had what I later learned were "gauges" in her earlobes. I did what I had done many times. I took her aside and told her I had heard what a great employee she was and a terrific Team Leader. I said I would like to know more about her but wanted her to know she had a future in this business. She expressed her appreciation for the compliments. I then said, in passing, that it would be best if she could "tone down" some of the things in her unique appearance.

To my surprise, Amanda looked at me right in the eye and in a very courteous and nondefensive way said she hoped I would reconsider my position and look at our customers. She said I might have noticed that most of our customers had tattoos and piercings, and she hoped I would open my mind to the possibility that it was time to change our appearance guidelines. Now this was an eighteen-year-old girl talking to the company president. She did not know me. She had just met me. Yet she made her point with maturity beyond her years. I told her I would take her suggestion "under advisement" and think about it.

Now, the rest of the story. I agreed with Matt that we should offer Amanda an Assistant Manager position and give her a substantial raise on the condition she quit her other jobs and work for us full time. She accepted. After just a few months, we asked her to take a position as manager of a store we were going to remodel and convert to a slightly different concept. We wanted her to open the new store as the manager. She did just that and executed one of the best store openings we had ever had.

Several months into her tenure as a store manager, I called and asked if I could come by and just chat with her. We arranged a time, sat down, and I asked her to tell me her story. She said she did not have much of a story but I encouraged her to just give me the outline of her upbringing and life. What a story! Both of Amanda's parents were drug abusers. They were not together most of the time. From the age of eight, Amanda had the responsibility of raising her younger brother. She had a couple of other siblings. The one steady influence in her life was her grandfather. She periodically lived with him when her parents were not functional. She recalled her grandfather bragging to his Navy veteran friends about the great tattoos Amanda had.

Amanda was a wonderful student and an avid reader. She was clearly above average in intelligence (both intellectual and emotional). She had a sense of responsibility to compensate for the lack of responsibility she had seen from both of her parents. She did not use drugs or abuse alcohol. She was a survivor. I knew more about her from that thirty-minute discussion than the two years she had worked for us.

It Takes Just One Person to Be a "Game Changer" in the Life of Another

Fast forward to later on: Amanda had a child, a beautiful little girl. While that was not exactly what I would have wished for her, she was an excellent mother. She purchased a house which she shared with her brother and his girlfriend. They were a family. They shared everything. They looked out for each other. Amanda bought a new car, paid off all her credit cards, had a savings account and an emergency fund.

From a business standpoint, Amanda was our most accomplished manager. She was always open to coaching and rarely made the same mistake twice. She was an excellent model for her employees, and I often got notes and letters from her customers about what a joy she was to meet and interact with. I loved that she loved her job. She often told me about her friends who hated their jobs and bosses, and she loved both. She put a smile on my face whenever I walked into her store.

Amanda was more than surviving. She was thriving and being a wonderful model for her employees, her brother and his family, as well as to her daughter. Where might she have landed, given her upbringing? Where might she have "fallen off the rails"? Did her family tree change? I think so! So often we learn that it takes just one person to be the "game changer" in the lives of others. Can you be that "game changer" in the life of one of your employees?

UPDATE: We sold the store to Amanda as part of my retirement plan. She has done exceptionally well, paid off the sales contract and renewed a lease, funded her retirement, and established an education fund for her daughter. She is rocking!

THE LESSONS:

- **Do not be blinded by your own prejudices. Focus on skills, character, and talent and not first impressions.**
- **Learn the stories of your good people. They will help you understand their currency as well as their strengths.**

Questions to Ponder

Are there talented people you have overlooked because they don't fit your preconceived ideas about what talent looks like?

Do you have subordinate managers who rely on certain team members and you don't know them at all?

Who on your team should you be aware of?

NOTES

(Your Own Observations)

"Coach" or . . . "Know it all"?

The best example of good management technique that builds a culture of listening and respect is one a consultant taught me. I was lucky enough to engage this important mentor at a critical time in our company's development.

Managers often answer questions from their good people, their "#2s", too quickly. After all, they are managers because they know stuff that their subordinates don't. Also, when a subordinate asks a question of a manager, the manager's instincts tell them to give the answer and do it fast! Why not? There are times when urgency demands a quick response. The fact is, those urgent times are very rare. We have found that in most cases, when a staff member asks a manager or supervisor a question (in a non-urgent circumstance), the best response is "What do you think?" or "How do you want to handle it?"

For many team members, given their upbringing and previous experience, being asked to contribute a solution, even in a safe and careful way, is very uncomfortable. We have seen people totally frozen with fear at the idea they are asked to produce any solution. They are so accustomed to just doing what they are told, often to avoid terrible consequences. They just cannot respond to the question "What do you think we should do?"

In general, I am an optimist. I believe most people who may not be comfortable with this kind of scenario can develop solution abilities over time. It takes a manager or supervisor with patience and wisdom to give them the tools to develop good problem-solving skills. These are lifelong skills. They are the skills that can make an enormous difference in a person's life and their "family tree".

Don't Be So Quick to Give an Answer

What are some of the techniques that can help a manager or supervisor bring out the problem-solving skills in their people? Primarily, ask the question and listen! Do not be too quick to give an answer just because you were asked. In fact, your people should grow so accustomed to producing solutions that they don't expect you to just pop back with the answer. It takes time and consistency, but you are looking for the following advancement in *problem-solving skills:*

1. The employee comes to you with direct questions, and you ask them their ideas for solutions. (Builds mutual respect and a culture of inclusion at the lowest levels.)

2. The employee comes to you with a problem and volunteers a solution that may or may not be great but is a start. (Don't discourage them by just dismissing the solution but rather suggest "that is one way but you might want to think about this…".)

3. The employee comes to you with a problem and a solution, seeking your approval of their solution. (They are beginning to become accountable for solving problems they see or have been identified and are becoming accountable and ready to act independently!)

4. The employee comes to you with a problem and how they solved it! (They have become totally accountable and are more than likely able to use the same technique with their subordinates!)

It is a mistake to believe that you can just skip to step 4 without witnessing the subordinate's comfort in making decisions. In some cases, jumping too quickly to 3. or 4. can overwhelm the subordinate because they have not built self-confidence to have that kind of independence. In a few cases, the subordinate is ready to jump to 4. but lacks the judgment or experience to make great decisions on their own.

Why don't more managers and supervisors (and owners!) use these techniques? I believe it is because one of the highest compliments we are paid is when someone asks our advice. It is a huge ego stroke! Young managers are particularly susceptible to yielding to the temptation of answering every question that comes their way. They are seeking affirmation that they are the right person for the job and are respected by their subordinates, peers, and bosses. The irony is that respect and affirmations come when their subordinates and peers see them truly empowering their team. The word "Empowerment" is thrown around a lot in management circles, but it is my experience that there is little done that leads to true empowerment. The technique described does a couple of things: It begins the empowerment process AND it demonstrates true respect and listening to the very people we value!

A FRONT LINE TALE

In the case of a law firm, a senior partner was tired of subordinates coming to him for advice. He had confidence these younger attorneys were capable and generally knew the right thing to do. They would take up his time asking questions that he needed them to resolve on their own. Why did they seek his advice? It could be due to their not wanting to make a mistake, or trying to save their own time, or maybe just out of habit. In any case, the senior partner started asking "What do you think?" before offering up the answer. Eventually, the younger attorneys would check with the senior partner after the fact. But, in another case, one of the junior partners came to the senior partner with a question that needed a quick answer. The junior partner said to the senior partner, "Don't ask me what I think. I know you know this right off the top of your head. If I had time, I would research it on my own. I just need the answer now!"

Obviously, the senior partner had done an excellent job of letting go of the need to be the answer man.

THE LESSONS:

- **Start asking your people for their solutions when they come to you with a question or problem, recognizing this may be a scary thing for them.**
- **Encourage people to take initiative when they show good decision-making.**
- **Do not give too much authority to a person who has failed to show good judgment.**

Questions to Ponder

How quick are you to provide an answer to a subordinate's question?

Do you have team members who are afraid of making a decision? How do you coach and counsel them?

Do you have team members who take too much initiative without showing good judgment?

What can you do to reel them back?

NOTES

(Your Own Observations)

Delegation Is Not A Simple Act!

While reviewing notes from leadership seminars I've attended over the years, one insight jumped out at me—and it is too valuable not to share. **Delegation**, when done well, is a powerful tool for development, motivation, and team growth. But when it is managed poorly, it leads to frustration, missed deadlines, and disappointed expectations—for both the leader and the employee.

If you want delegation to work, you must approach it *deliberately.* Here are some key principles that can turn delegation into a success instead of a setback:

1. Choose the Right Person

Select someone who *wants* the task—and who has (or can develop) the skills to do it well. Do not just drop a job on someone who's reluctant or overwhelmed. You might need to explain what is in it for them:

- A chance to learn something new
- More variety in their role
- The opportunity to display a hidden talent
- A meaningful contribution to the team

Check their willingness *before* assigning the responsibility.

2. Share ALL the Information—and Then Some

Few things are more frustrating than being asked to do a task without the proper info. Do not make them come back to you six times asking for bits and pieces. Take the time to explain:

- The full scope of the job
- Who else is involved
- Where the necessary resources are

- What success looks like

If anything, **over-communicate.**

3. Negotiate a Realistic Deadline

Inexperienced team members often set deadlines that are too optimistic. They do not yet understand all the steps involved. Ask for their timeline then coach them toward a more realistic one. Agree on a final deadline together—and build in some breathing room if you can.

4. Check In—but Do Not Take Over

Midway through the task, check progress. Ask:

- "Do you have what you need?"
- "Any roadblocks?"
- "Still feeling confident about the deadline?"

Resist the urge to jump in and take over. Your job is to **coach,** not to **rescue.** Offer help, ask good questions, and give them space to figure it out. This is how people grow.

5. Show Gratitude

Once the job is done, say thank you. **Genuinely.** A lack of appreciation is one of the fastest ways to make someone think twice before taking on more responsibility. Gratitude fuels growth.

6. Learn from the Outcome

Do not judge someone's potential based solely on how their *first* delegated task turns out. Look at how they managed the challenge:

- Did they ask good questions?
- Did they learn from missteps?

- Were they accountable?
- Did they show signs of growth?

Use that insight to decide whether to delegate again—and how much more they might be ready for next time.

Real-World Delegation Examples

Consider breaking out tasks that do not have to stay on your plate:

- **Marketing materials:** Setup, take-down, storage, communication with the team.
- **Maintenance routines:** Backroom standards, equipment, upkeep, checklists.
- **Event prep or training roles:** Let someone own a monthly meeting topic or lead a training demo.

In any case, **make it official.** Give people the appropriate authority and communicate their new role clearly to the team. Recognition makes all the difference.

THE LESSONS:

- **Delegation is not just about offloading work. It is about growing your people.**
- **It is a leadership skill—and a development opportunity.**
- **Do it thoughtfully. Do it with intention.**

Questions to Ponder

How good are you at effective delegation? How can you improve?

Do you check in with your team members who have accepted a delegated job, BEFORE the deadline?

Are you good at providing all of the necessary information for the team member to complete the job?

NOTES

(Your Own Observations)

When They Ask for a Raise—What Your Employees Should Hear

Every now and then, I would visit one of our stores and have a team member pull me aside—usually someone young, confident, and curious. If they were feeling bold enough, they'd ask: **"Mr. Schauermann, I've worked here for over nine months… how do I get a raise?"**

Honestly, this question would catch me off guard. When I was sixteen or seventeen, I wouldn't have dreamed of asking the company owner something like that. But here's what I love about it: young team members will ask what older employees are often thinking—but might never say aloud.

And that makes this question incredibly important. If we're serious about creating a *wholesome and supportive workplace*, we owe it to our teams to provide a **clear, respectful, and useful answer.**

Here's What I Told the Last Employee Who Asked (Let Us Call Him Bill):

"Bill, that is a great question. Let me give you two ways to approach it.

"First, just go to your manager and ask, 'What do I have to do to get a raise?' That is a totally fair question. And if you ask it respectfully and in private, you should expect an honest answer—even if it is not the one you hoped for.

"Second—and this is the approach I *really* recommend—grab your performance criteria from orientation, then go to your manager and ask, 'Sally, where do I need to improve to be worth more to the company?' If she can't give you a clear answer (maybe she needs time to review your performance first), that's a sign something's off. And you're well within your rights to ask for a follow-up meeting with her and her boss to get a proper, thoughtful response."

Managers, Are You Ready for This Conversation?

You should be. Being able to clearly answer this question is a **core part of leading a team with integrity.**

Here are a few truths worth keeping in mind:

Wages are not just about time served. Ideally, yes, raises would flow consistently based on time and performance—but real-world compensation is more complex. Raises are influenced by:

- o The **employee's performance and contribution**
- o The **store's profitability**
- o The **local labor market**
- o The **company's broader economic position**

  - **Outstanding performers should be rewarded.** I have heard managers say, "We can't afford to give them a raise." I say: **"Bunk."** There is *always* room in labor costs for someone who is consistently bringing value to the team. Even in a low- or no-profit store, **we are not being smart** if we let our best people walk away because we didn't recognize their efforts.
  - **Requests for raises are a signal.** If someone is asking for more money, it might mean it's time to do a **full team evaluation.** Chances are others are wondering about their value too. A consistent, thoughtful evaluation system, like our **Performance Evaluation Form** (Appendix 2) helps ensure fairness, rewards, and coaching are based on real data—not just gut feelings.

Beyond Wages: What Really Keeps People

At the end of the day, pay is only one part of the puzzle. We have seen over and over again that employees stick around and *thrive* when four key things are present:

1. A boss who **respects them**
2. **Coworkers** who are fun and dependable
3. A **sense of purpose**—that their work makes a difference
4. A strong feeling of **fairness** on the job

If those four things are **missing**, no raise in the world will keep someone happy.

If those four things are **present**, most people will not even ask for more money—*as long as we stay competitive with the market.*

THE LESSONS:

- **Managers should always be ready to respond with a fair and thoughtful answer when a team member asks about a raise.**
- **Use these moments as an opportunity to listen, evaluate, and support growth.**

And remember—regular team assessments help you stay ahead of these conversations and ensure your best people feel seen, valued, and rewarded.

Questions to Ponder

Are you ready to answer the tough questions about pay?

Do you do overall staff evaluations to stay on top of the good people who don't ask about a raise but deserve one?

Do you honestly give feedback to your underperforming team members so they have a chance to improve and know their standing on the team?

Do you tend to reward the squeaky wheel rather than the top performers?

Are there team members who aren't worth what they were when you last gave them a raise? Have their life circumstances changed or are they ready for a change in jobs?

NOTES

(Your Own Observations)

FAIR TREATMENT

Responding to Employee Concerns the Right Way

A conversation with one of our managers surfaced a challenge we've all faced at some point:

> ***What do you do when a crew member brings you a concern about something that happened when you were not there?***

Do you act on it immediately? Do you launch an investigation? How do you manage it fairly—without ignoring potential problems or violating anyone's rights? It is a tough position to be in, but there *is* a thoughtful, fair approach that aligns with our values and our Fair Treatment Policy (Appendix 3). Here is how to navigate it.

Step One: Consider the Source

Start by asking yourself this critical question: **Is the person bringing the issue a *first party* to the situation?** (Did they *personally witness* or were they *directly involved* in the event?)

☑ **If Yes (First-Party Information):**

You must engage the **Fair Treatment Policy.**

- **Bring all parties involved into a joint meeting.**
- **Make sure everyone has a chance to tell their side, face-to-face.** You will be amazed how perspectives shift when people are asked to speak openly in front of one another. This approach takes a bit more time, but it saves hours of second-guessing and

confusion later. It also **prevents misunderstandings**, builds mutual respect, and keeps gossip from spreading unchecked.

☑ **If No (Second- or Third-Party Information):**

Manage it differently. This type of information demands caution.

- **It might be valid—or it might be inaccurate, self-serving, or coming from someone who thrives on drama.**
- **Do not take immediate action based solely on hearsay.** Instead, do a **quiet, broad check-in.**

Step Two: Quietly Take the Pulse

Here is how to gather context **without stirring the pot:**

1. **Check in directly** with the person who was affected.
    - Ask broad questions like, "How are things going?" or "Is there anything that's made you uncomfortable lately?"
    - Let them know about our **Harassment and Discrimination Policy**, the **Hotline**, and how seriously we take a safe and respectful environment
2. **Talk to a couple of trusted Team Leaders.**
    - Keep the questions general: "Have you noticed anything that seemed off or inappropriate?"
    - Do *not* name names or suggest where the information came from.

This helps you gauge the **overall culture and atmosphere** in the store when you are not around.

3. **Educate, do not accuse.**
    - Whether you find anything or not, take the opportunity to reinforce expectations.

- Team Leaders should know what to do if they ever observe or hear something inappropriate.
- Consider holding a quick **crew meeting** to go over workplace rights and responsibilities and remind the team what to do when they face difficult situations.

Step Three: Handle Discipline with Care

If you confirm that inappropriate behavior has occurred:

- **Do not assume guilt** without giving everyone the chance to speak.
- If a Fair Treatment Meeting is warranted, it should happen **before** conclusions are drawn.
- If discipline is needed, manage it **privately**—especially in cases involving a Team Leader or peer-to-peer conflict. Public discipline often creates shame rather than accountability.

A FRONT LINE TALE

A Manager Gets Accused

One of the most difficult challenges I faced was when I received a phone call from an irate parent of one of our minor employees. She was outraged that we had employed a manager who was talking about very inappropriate topics with her son. The manager was a recent hire. She was married and I had not met her husband. The caller said that her son and some of his coworkers were at her house talking about the manager's approach to the young man, as well as her approaches to the young girls who worked at the unit. The accusations were so serious it demanded action.

It would have been easy to just ask the manager about the various accusations and I would have assumed she would deny them. Then where are we? If we were a large company, we would have called in our Human Resources department to investigate. I decided to do an internal investigation. The first step was to interview the young man whose mother had called me. I wanted to know exactly what was happening in the store to him. I didn't want information about others, just his first-hand experience. I asked him not to talk with others about the investigation and I needed to know any others with whom he thought I should talk. I then interviewed two additional people who had firsthand experience.

The next step was to sit with the accused manager. I explained some rather serious accusations had been made about her behavior. I was willing to conduct a face-to-face with one or more of the accusers but wanted her response first. She said she would talk to me the next day and she arrived with her husband. They were livid that we had talked to employees without her having a chance to share her side of the story. I made it clear that was what this meeting was for. I again told her I would be willing to have the accusing employee(s) sit with us. She refused and chose to resign at that time.

Sexual harassment, racist accusations, and other discriminatory behaviors require a little more tact and confidentiality than just personality conflicts. There are many seminars and workshops devoted to how to conduct internal investigations. The challenge of dealing with a manager vs. employee conflict also demands tact and confidentiality. In the case of this manager accused of unwelcome sexual approaches, her resignation was a relief. The evidence was overwhelming.

Employee-to-Employee Conflict

More than once, in the restaurant industry, conflict arises between two employees. Some managers make the decision to just not schedule them together. Often, just taking some time to sit them down, face-to-face, to air their apparent grievances creates not just a "No War Zone" but a work environment where there is mutual respect and understanding. It really is amazing how stories change when people are sitting in the same room where they are accusing each other of unfair biases, and/or unspoken agendas. Of course, this approach takes time but the payoff can be fantastic—preservation of two good employees and an easier time planning schedules.

THE LESSONS:

- **Fair treatment means listening to everyone involved—not making assumptions based on one side of the story.**
- **It means being proactive without being reactive, respectful without being dismissive, and always choosing clarity over convenience.**
- **When in doubt, ask yourself: "Would I feel this was fair if I were the person being talked about?"**

That is how you build trust, maintain morale, and keep your store a respectful place to work.

Questions to Ponder

Are there unresolved conflicts between working peers? Might they be resolved in a face-to-face session?

As a manager or owner, what kind of conflicts do you avoid or procrastinate dealing with? How can you improve in this area?

Do you listen to some team members who complain about others and discount the complaining of others on your team?

NOTES
(Your Own Observations)

PROGRESSIVE DISCIPLINE

Discipline and Documentation: Leading with Clarity and Respect

One principle I have come to deeply value is this:

> ***A known quantity—flawed though they may be—is often better than the unknown person you might bring in as a replacement.***

Let us be honest: **no one is perfect**, certainly not myself. But I choose to believe that most people genuinely want to do a good job. The key is understanding that people define a "good job" differently. That is where leadership comes in. Our responsibility is not to replace that motivation—it's to **unleash** it by clearly defining what excellence looks like and what's expected.

The Power of Clear Expectations and Follow-Up

When performance issues arise, **verbal conversations alone are not enough.** People hear only about 40 percent of what's said. Our brains filter and reframe information quickly, especially in stressful or emotional moments. That is why we use **follow-up letters** after serious performance conversations with managers and Team Leaders.

These letters serve several critical purposes:

- They **document what was discussed** in detail.
- They reinforce **what the expectations are** moving forward.
- They outline **what will happen** if those expectations are not met.

- They highlight **what support** we, as leaders, are committed to providing.

We tell the employee or manager upfront:

"You will be receiving a follow-up letter that summarizes our conversation. If anything is in the letter that we *did not* discuss, call us right away. If there is anything we *did* discuss that's missing, also reach out for clarification.

A FRONT LINE TALE

Years ago, I had a serious discussion with a manager regarding **falsified payroll records** involving a long-term employee. This was a **"First and Last Warning"** conversation—non-negotiable and clear. Afterwards, she received the expected follow-up letter and immediately called me, upset that this incident was now officially documented.

I asked her two questions:

1. "Is there anything in the letter that we didn't talk about?"
2. "Is there anything we talked about that's not in the letter?"

She paused and said she would think about it. A couple of days later, she called back—her tone had shifted. She said she "got it." Seeing everything laid out on paper made it real for her. She was shaken, but more importantly, she was *motivated.* That same manager went on to work with me for **fifteen more years.**

Why Letters Work Better than Write-Ups

Could I have just done a "write-up" instead of a letter? Sure. But those are often too clinical, too impersonal. They do not spark **real reflection** or show **real investment** in a person's growth.

A letter says:

"I care enough about your success to not only have the hard conversation—but also to take the time to make sure you're fully equipped to improve."

I have used this method not just for major issues, but also for **smaller performance gaps**, when I really wanted someone to understand **how much their actions matter.** If their behavior is not important enough to address clearly and personally, then **what message are we sending?**

The Manager's Responsibility

Good managers and leaders do not fear candid conversations. They see them as an opportunity to coach, correct, and build trust.

Every follow-up letter should include:

- ☑ A clear description of the **unacceptable behavior or issue**
- ☑ The **consequences** if the behavior does not change
- ☑ The **support or assistance** you are willing to provide to help the change happen

If any of those three are missing, the job is not done. (See Appendix 3)

THE LESSONS:

- **Discipline is not punishment—it is leadership.**
- **The goal is not to "catch" people failing, but to give them every chance to succeed.**

- **The best way to do that is through clarity, consistency, and communication, especially in writing.**

Questions to Ponder

Do you hesitate writing issues down because you lack good writing skills?

Do you hesitate documenting poor or critical performance shortcomings because then you may actually have to do something if they don't improve?

What history do you have regarding documentation that may influence your hesitancy to use it?

NOTES

(Your Own Observations)

From Coaching to Personnel Action for Line Employees

In our company, we believed that **discipline is a tool for growth—not punishment.** The goal was not to "catch" employees doing something wrong, but to **correct behavior** in a way that was constructive, clear, and respectful.

Here is how our progressive discipline process worked:

1. Verbal Coaching & Positive Reinforcement

The foundation of our performance culture: **on-the-floor engagement.**

- Managers must be **actively present**—noticing great work and providing praise publicly when appropriate.
- At the same time, coaching and correcting should happen privately, one-on-one, in a calm and supportive tone.
- This consistent feedback loop helps team members grow and understand expectations early.

Reminder: Praise is most powerful in public. Correction is most effective in private.

2. Formal Performance Appraisals

In addition to day-to-day coaching, we used **formal evaluations** to highlight strengths, identify gaps, and create accountability.

- An employee's **first performance appraisal** should happen within the **first 60 days** of employment.
- After that, appraisals must happen **at least annually**, or **more frequently** when performance needs more active attention.
- Use the **evaluation form** provided at hire (See Appendix 2) as your guide.

- If the employee's behavior or performance is slipping, the written appraisal may serve as a **wake-up call**—often correcting issues before they escalate.

☑ Tip: Use a calendar or scheduling tool to stay on track with appraisals. (See Appendix 2)

3. Personnel Action Form (PAF)

The **Personnel Action Form** is a serious step and is used when:

- A **severe violation occurs** (e.g., theft, drugs/alcohol use, threats, or physical altercations),

  OR

- Coaching and performance evaluations have **not resulted in change**, and performance remains below standard.

A key sign that it is time to use the PAF:

You catch yourself saying, "If this happens one more time, I'm going to fire them."

That is when it's time to have a **direct and clear meeting** with the employee—a "line in the sand" conversation.

The meeting should include:

- A clear summary of the **unsatisfactory behavior or performance**
- What **must change**, by **when**
- What consequences will be if change doesn't occur (e.g., suspension or termination)
- A **signed copy** of the PAF, acknowledging receipt and understanding. (Appendix 3–the correct form and documentation.)

This Process Is about Change—Not "Checking Boxes"

Too many organizations treat progressive discipline as nothing more than a formality to protect themselves from legal risk. That was not our approach.

Our goal was to help people succeed.

If a manager is using this process just to "build a case" to terminate, it is time to step back and **reexamine the coaching culture** in the store.

THE LESSONS:

Progressive discipline is not a punishment system. It is a leadership tool, designed to:

- **Change behavior to an acceptable standard.**
- **Provide clear, written communication.**
- **Support employee growth!**
- **Protect the organization legally, when needed.**

If done consistently and sincerely, this process not only develops better team members—it creates better leaders.

Questions to Ponder

What are your biggest obstacles to doing performance reviews?

Do you have clearly defined expectations so you can be perfectly clear about the job?

Do you think evaluations are just a "legal requirement" to protect the company?

What positive things might come out of doing regular written performance reviews?

NOTES

(Your Own Observations)

CHOICES

Bringing Our People to Conscious Choices through Conversation and Documentation

In today's world, people face more choices than ever—how they live, work, and connect. That freedom also shows up in the workplace where people choose how they show up, how they engage, and how they grow—or do not.

Our job as leaders is no longer about simply *directing* people. It is about helping them see the **choices available** to them and guiding them toward ones that serve both their personal growth and the organization's goals.

The Power of Conscious Choice

Choice-making is a learned skill. Some employees come to us having never been encouraged to think through their decisions or understand the consequences. Our role is to **coach them to clarity.**

When managers shift from "telling" to helping people choose, something powerful happens:

- Employees feel **empowered**, not micromanaged.
- The organization sees more **accountable, engaged** behavior.
- Managers gain clarity, reduce drama, and increase their influence.

Why Managers Avoid Talking about Choices

Here are three common reasons managers avoid open choice conversations:

Uncertainty – They don't know what options the employee has.

Responsibility – They believe it is *their job* to make the choice (and bear the consequences).

Fear – They worry the employee might choose something that hurts in the short term (like quitting).

Avoidance leads to stress, inconsistency, and even legal trouble. Clear communication around **choices and consequences** creates better outcomes for everyone.

A Real-World Example: Tardiness

Let us walk through a typical issue:

Traditional Approach

- Verbal and written warnings, maybe a suspension.
- Termination follows if the pattern continues.
- Result: The employee might not show before being fired, and resentment or legal risk can follow.

Avoidance Approach

- The manager tolerates lateness to avoid being short-staffed.
- Other employees get frustrated.
- Eventually, the manager fires the employee in a moment of frustration.
- Result: A claim of discrimination or inconsistency.

Choice Point Approach

After the **second** tardy incident, the manager sits with the employee and outlines clear options:

> "You have some choices here. Let us go through them together."

A. You can choose to quit—punctuality is not your strength, and that's okay.

B. You can commit to change and show us you are serious.

C. You can commit, but if the behavior continues, you are telling us you're not ready, and that it will likely lead to termination.

D. You can acknowledge the challenge, give it your best, and if it does not improve, you'll resign with notice.

This simple shift in approach does a few things:

- **Centers responsibility** with the employee.
- **Reduces conflict** and surprises later.
- **Builds trust and transparency** with the rest of the team.
- **Develops life skills**—many employees have never had a manager walk them through consequences like this.

Documenting Choices

We often see documentation as a legal formality—"CYA" paperwork to protect the company. While that is important, it's not the only reason to write things down.

Documentation should also:

- **Support behavior change.**
- **Clarify understanding** (since verbal conversations can be misremembered).

- **Capture choices made**—and the consequences the employee agreed to.

Example: Instead of saying, "Written warning for tardiness," document, elaborate: "We reviewed four choices. Employee chose Option B: commit to improved punctuality, understanding continued tardiness may lead to termination."

This puts the **focus on growth**, not just punishment—and helps prevent miscommunication down the road.

Can This Work for Managers Too?

Absolutely—but with nuance.

Supervisors often hesitate to bring Choice Points to underperforming managers (Less-Than-Satisfactory or "LTS" performers) because:

- The stakes are higher.
- The impact of losing a manager is more severe.
- The conversations feel more personal or uncomfortable.

Still, when a manager is struggling, **supervisors must not compensate.** Otherwise, they become "maintenance managers" themselves—propping up weak performance instead of building a formidable team.

A Supervisor's Choice Point Conversation with a Manager Might Sound Like:

> "You're facing some options here, and I want to support you in choosing what's best—for you *and* for the team."

Choices for the Manager:

A. Ignore feedback and face poor reviews, smaller raises, and stalled growth.

B. Keep trying the same approach and getting the same results.

C. Try something new—ask for help, take training, or change your leadership strategy.

Choices for the Supervisor:

A. Accept the LTS performance as permanent (and grow resentful).

B. Escalate to formal documentation and prepare for termination.

C. Have a transparent, supportive conversation that emphasizes the manager's ability to improve and own the outcome.

Find the Currency

Every employee—and manager—has a personal currency: something they value.

It could be:

- Time off
- Recognition
- Autonomy
- Job security
- Promotion potential
- Less oversight

Great leaders tie expectations and feedback to that currency:

> "Right now, this issue is standing in the way of [the thing you value]. I would like to help you fix it."

THE LESSONS:

Every person in your organizational staff, managers, and supervisors has choices to make. When those choices are clearly presented, people are more likely to:

- **Take ownership of their behavior.**
- **Move from a victim mindset to a growth mindset.**
- **Contribute to a culture of accountability and mutual respect.**

The outcome? A stronger team, less drama, better retention, and a workplace where people are growing—not just grinding.

Questions to Ponder

What is the biggest obstacle for you to use this "choice" approach to performance?

What do you fear when thinking about using this approach with employees? With managers?

How can you determine what an employee or manager's currency is?

NOTES

(Your Own Observations)

WHAT DO SUCCESSFUL MANAGERS DO?

Successful Managers:

A) Develop people.

B) Learn how to bond with people.

C) Model the work ethic.

D) Influence behavior of the team.

E) Are Motivation Experts who generate pride by making demands, encouraging their team.

F) Treat people with respect.

G) Build Team Spirit, a feeling of togetherness.

H) Are great Time Managers.

Specific things successful managers do each day:

- Say hello.
- Talk to people.
- Compliment people.
- Jump in and help.
- Ask for ideas.
- Keep the crew informed of all sorts of stuff, even stuff they don't have to know.

A Few Notes on Time Management

Early in my career, I was a lousy manager of my time. In fact, my boss signed me up for a seminar on time management, and I forgot to go! He made me pay for it out of my meager salary. I finally went to one that really rang my bell. The most crucial factor for me was learning to merge my calendars for work and personal life.

Calendars and phones are great tools but...Time Management involves more than just getting dates down on a screen. Our time is a precious asset. If we are spending it on less than vital, important tasks, we are wasting it!

Understanding how to prioritize all that can consume time is so important to create value and to have a quality of life while still accomplishing long-term goals. Paper and pen can really help a manager set their priorities properly and make real progress that is meaningful to their organization, as well as for them personally.

Using a yellow pad or your note tool on your computer, start writing down the things that are on your to-do list. This list should include both work/business items as well as personal demands. Don't worry about putting them in any kind of order. Some of them have deadlines that must be met and those should be noted. Some of them are longer-term personal goals or projects. Use a priority marking system. I recommend noting beside every item on the list whether it is an "A", "B", "C" or "D" item. An "A" is a vital, critical task or event. A "B" is important, but not necessarily vital. It may be imposed by a boss, a customer, or government authority. It must be done but is not necessarily vital to accomplish your long-term goals. A "C" is one of those tasks that would be nice but isn't pressing or critical to your long-term goals. A "D" is one of those items that appears, but in the grand scope of things is not vital, important, or even closely related to your personal goals. It may have been put on the list because someone else asked you to do it. The sooner you can eliminate those items, the better.

Once every item is labeled with a letter it is time to begin to build your real task/to-do list with a schedule. Looking at the "A" items, select the most vital, critical one and make it "A1". The next one is "A2" and so forth. Do the same with the "B" and "C" items, beginning with B1, B2, B3, etc. When you get to the "D" items, decide whether to take them off the list, pass them to someone else, or move them up in priority.

You may find that a task like "A2" requires a couple of steps to accomplish. This is where you can have a huge impact on your effectiveness in the long term. Consider the steps required and note them. Go to your calendar and beginning with "A1" schedule the beginning steps. Be realistic about how much time it will take to accomplish them. Do the same with every "A" item, then "B" item and "C" item. You can build the deadlines into your schedule at this time. A couple of things may become clear. You may see that you have more time to accomplish the important goals and tasks. You may find yourself over-scheduled and need to spread out some of the tasks to a more reasonable framework. In time, you may find that what you thought was vital or important really isn't after all.

If you have been honest about your personal to-do list along with your business/work list, you will begin to see where one or the other has been sacrificed in the past. Family, marriage, children, parents, friends are important relationships to preserve and nurture. A failure to incorporate those goals and tasks will result in a distortion in your priorities.

On the next page is a list of tasks/to-dos from my own personal calendar with substeps and calendar entries.

PRIORITY:	ITEM:	DATE SET:
B3	Do performance review of Dave	5/15
	Prep PA documents	5/12
C1	Mow lawn before family party	5/4
A3	Consider Graduate school	6/30
	Look at options for schools	5/20
	Make list of tasks to qualify	5/25
	Study for GMAT	6/15-10/20
A4	Get financing for Kitsap remodel	7/1
B2	Go to Jonathan's concert	5/12 8:00PM
B1	Order new freezer for Tacoma	NOW!
A2	Draft letter to Kathy, re: performance review	5/1
	Send Kathy letter	5/2
A5	Talk to Bret about management at Everett	5/24
A1	Get Barb birthday present	6/2
C3	Replace filters on furnace	5/30
B4	Shop for new car for Barb	6/1-6/30
C2	Get a haircut	5/3
B5	Talk to Matt about new bonus proposal	5/15
B6	Publish Financials for May	5/5
B7	Bridge party	5/7, 7:00 PM

In this case, I have already eliminated my "D" tasks.

THE LESSONS:

- **Success comes from the actions you take, not the theories you read. Do the things that lead to success!**
- **Make sure you acknowledge both work and personal goals/ dates etc. in your time management system.**

Questions to Ponder

Are you a "Successful Manager"? What is missing?

What part of managing time is your biggest challenge?

NOTES

(Your Own Observations)

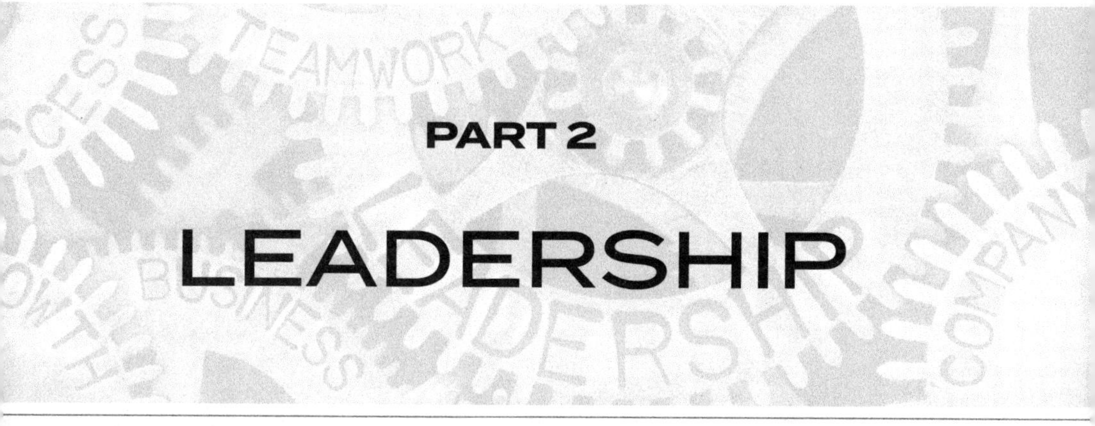

PART 2

LEADERSHIP

LEADERSHIP DESCRIBED

For the purposes of this book, *Leadership* is defined as ***the ability to create an environment where team members and staff feel motivated, valued, and inspired.*** True leadership helps perpetuate the culture of the organization for the benefit of customers, guests, employees, vendors, and the greater community.

Leadership, as opposed to management, is a long-term, visionary skill set. It requires consistency and a deep understanding of the organization's goals—often stretching far beyond the immediate future. Great leadership cultivates the next generation of leaders. My family and I experienced the impact of exceptional leadership firsthand—through compassion and listening that went beyond anything we ever expected from a large organization.

A FRONT LINE TALE

Anne Beiler, known more widely as "Auntie Anne," of Hand-Rolled Soft Pretzels fame, began her company in a farmer's market in Lancaster County, Pennsylvania. Over time, she built it into a thriving chain with over one thousand corporate and franchised locations before eventually selling it. In 1993, our company was fortunate to open the first Auntie Anne's franchise stores in the Pacific Northwest.

Anne spoke at numerous national conventions celebrating women in business and appeared on many national and local television programs. Her commitment to people was well-documented, and a sizable portion of her profits supported causes in her local community and across the nation. She is, without question, a true hero.

What many did not know were the personal stories that illustrated Anne's unwavering attitude of *"Others before self."* My wife and I experienced that generosity during one of the most difficult years of our lives.

In March of 1995, our fourteen-year-old son was diagnosed with a serious illness. His treatment required at least one week in the hospital every four weeks for the next six months. During that time, our full attention needed to be on him and on our twelve-year-old daughter. We were also preparing to open our third Auntie Anne's location along with another restaurant that summer. Clearly, I was in no shape to lead those efforts. Thankfully, our Vice President of Operations, Bret, stepped up and ensured that both openings went off smoothly.

That year, I was unable to attend Auntie Anne's annual franchisee convention. Bret went in my place and shared our situation with Anne. Despite her many responsibilities running a rapidly growing national brand, Anne began a weekly routine that deeply touched our family: Every Monday morning, she called us. From Pennsylvania or wherever she happened to be, she reached out—not with scripted words or generic comfort, but with authentic concern.

Each week, I would hear, "Hello, this is Anne. How are you doing, Kurt? Tell me about Daniel. How is Barbara? What can I do for you? Remember, you are in our prayers at Auntie Anne's corporate office."

These were not just polite gestures; they were heartfelt, consistent, and deeply personal. Anne's compassion and care made a profound difference in our lives. Even today, her kindness still resonates with me. She embodies the very spirit of leadership that uplifts and empowers others. Who would not want to be part of an organization that demonstrates that kind of genuine care?

Retaining great managers—and franchisees for that matter—is not about policies or programs. It's about creating a culture where people feel they *belong*, and where their work *matters*. Anne's sincere outreach and her willingness to listen during our family's most vulnerable time turned me into an enthusiastic advocate for Auntie Anne's. Her compassion became my motivation—my currency.

It is my hope that more business leaders will recognize their role as something greater than simply achieving sales and profit targets. Of course, those goals are essential. But the role of a leader is also to enhance the lives of those they are entrusted with—team members, customers, vendors, partners, and co-owners alike.

That is the kind of leadership that lasts. That is the kind of leadership that changes lives.

CONFRONTING DIFFICULT ISSUES

Not all stories begin and end with wonderful conversations and then life goes on smoothly. Sometimes there are huge challenges for the people we work with as they deal with the chaos they may have grown up with or found themselves in.

A FRONT LINE TALE

This was the case with Kate. Kate was late for work again. She was the opening Team Leader at our Northgate Shopping Center store and had originally worked for us at a store in Eastern Washington. She called and said she had been in an accident the previous night and her car was towed. She needed help getting it out of impound. Nathan and I agreed to meet her at our office which was within walking distance of her apartment. When she came in, she looked terrible. She confessed she had been drinking and had hit a curb and her car stalled. A police officer came by, realized that she could not drive her car, saw a six-pack of beer on the floor of the car, and agreed to give her a ride home.

We were suspicious that Kate had a drinking problem and asked her if she thought that was the root cause of her issues. She didn't know what constituted a "drinking problem" but was willing to consider it. Nathan, her supervisor, took her to the impound lot and tried to get her car but it was "totaled" and not drivable. Kate burst into tears and said she did not remember anything about the accident—a classic blackout.

We asked her to undergo an alcohol evaluation and be willing to undergo treatment if it was recommended. She agreed. The evaluation came back saying she had an issue with alcohol but also had some other psychological issues that manifested themselves in her being a "cutter". This was a new one for me. After trying outpatient treatment, the counselors recommended an intensive in-patient treatment program. Kate completed twenty-eight days of treatment and although she had a few slips, she went into recovery from her addictions.

She was promoted to management and took on a tricky situation in a store in Eastern Washington near her birth home. I was proud of her. Kate was not a "superstar" manager, but she had been living a clean and sober life for six years when the store Kate was managing was sold and the new owner decided to go a different direction. Kate stayed sober, met her life partner, got married, and began working at a grocery store chain—a job she loved.

Humanizing Leadership

Kate's journey reminds us that employees aren't just workers—they're people with struggles, histories, and layers that often go unseen. By showing care and offering structured support, instead of punishment, we allowed her to confront her deeper issues and ultimately change the trajectory of her life.

Just like it was described in the Choices points chapter in Part 1, Management, Kate's situation was handled in a way that acknowledged her agency while also providing guidance. She was given the space to choose recovery and growth, not just job retention. That's long-term empowerment.

Recognizing and Addressing Underlying Issues

Kate's story beautifully illustrates how behavior (like tardiness or inconsistency) can be symptoms of something deeper—addiction, mental health struggles, trauma. Surface-level discipline would've missed the real problem entirely.

Real Leadership Is Messy and Brave

It would have been far easier to let Kate go early on, but we didn't. We took the harder routes, showing care, setting boundaries, and sticking with her. That is not just management. That is leadership with integrity. The joy we received from seeing her succeed personally and professionally was well worth it!

Sustainable Growth, Not Perfection

Kate didn't turn into a superstar, and she didn't have to. The goal wasn't perfection—it was progress, stability, and living a healthier, more honest life. That's a huge win in itself.

THE LESSONS:

- **A huge benefit and joy in being a leader of people and organizations is seeing your teammates flourish and grow from your coaching and influence.**
- **Rather than shy away from difficult situations, Managers and good leaders lean into them and display caring in real terms.**
- **Both the leader and the team member move from Victimhood to Empowerment.**

Questions to Ponder

Do you feel equipped to address issues that go beyond on-floor job performance?

What resources might you find to assist you?

What is the risk of raising deeply personal issues with team members?

What is the upside?

NOTES

(Your Own Observations)

LISTENING

The Key to True "Connection"!

Developing great listening skills becomes a key component of being that boss who your team members will remember long after they leave your employ, to being "Engaged" with them. Effective "employee engagement" requires leaders to really value their people, to really listen to them, because what they think and believe is important to the leader. What is influencing their behavior? What is their mind occupied with? What has their experience been with bosses, parents, teachers, coaches and other leaders? What are the things they value most? Rarely does a person value money first and foremost! It may be security, which usually involves money, but often their real currency is trust, loyalty, encouragement, and positive relationships.

Good listening starts with asking questions that require more than "Yes" or "No" answers. Many questions that cannot or should not be asked in the interview become fair game after a person has come on board with you. Questions about family history, children, boyfriends/girlfriends, and husbands or wives are openings to learning more about people and what makes them tick. Asking them directly who their best or worst boss was can be another opening question. Asking them the best part of a previous job also opens doors. Often after someone has been with you for a while they begin to trust you enough to share their career dreams and their life goals.

Connecting team members, managers and owners together has a value. The value is to ALL the parties, not just the business and the team members. Successful owners, managers, and team members are interested in being connected to the job beyond a paycheck. I remember going on business trips with my dad or wandering around the State Restaurant Show with him. He would engage in long conversations and be listening to all the people he knew from his time as a salesman. I would quickly become bored and move on and leave him to his "small talk" with his peers. What I did not understand was that it was his carefully nurtured personality that caused him to talk with and really listen to others. It paid off both socially and professionally in later years. He did not come by that trait by accident. He practiced it always and in all ways!

Sydney Harris, a longtime Chicago journalist once wrote, "The time to relax is when you don't have time for it." It could be similarly said, "The time to listen is when you don't have time for it!" Like so many other management skills, time spent listening saves time, aggravation, and disappointment later. It is not "Urgent" but it is "Vital"!

Determining If You Are Really Listening

What did you say? What did *they* say?

When I ask a manager or team member about a situation involving someone on their crew, a few things become immediately clear. Often, the response begins with, "Well, what I told him was..." or "I told her she needed to..."

My first question in return is simple: **"What did *they* say?"**

That's usually when things get quiet. The manager often can't recall what the employee said in response. They remember their own words clearly but draw a blank when it comes to the other person's. That's a red flag, a clear indicator that listening skills need work.

I struggled with this myself early in my career. I thought listening was just about nodding, maintaining eye contact, and repeating back what someone said. And while those techniques are useful, there's a deeper element that truly defines great listening.

Real listening means genuinely caring about the other person—not just trying to influence or manipulate them into doing what we want. It's about showing respect, not just extracting compliance.

If we want to engage our people, we must value them. That means being interested in *what they think* and *why they think it*. What's driving their behavior? What's occupying their mind? What are their past experiences with authority—bosses, parents, teachers, coaches? What do they truly value?

Spoiler: It's rarely just money.

Sure, people care about financial security—but their real "currency" is often trust, encouragement, loyalty, or a sense of belonging. When we listen to *those* things, we begin to understand what truly motivates our people—and that's when real engagement begins.

Obstacles to Listening

Despite the clear benefits of good listening, several common obstacles prevent managers and leaders from doing it well. Overcoming these challenges is essential to building trust, engagement, and a culture of excellence.

1. Time Constraints

Why don't we slow down and listen before jumping into our own agendas? The answer is simple: we're busy. As business owners and managers, we have a lot to accomplish—fast. Listening takes time, and urgent tasks often crowd out what's truly *vital*. But here's the paradox: while listening may not feel urgent, it *is* vital. In fact, time spent listening early prevents time spent cleaning up misunderstandings and mistakes later.

Listening is also discipline. To become an excellent leader, you must make it a non-negotiable part of who you are.

2. Past Experiences of Team Members

Your people don't show up as blank slates. They bring with them a lifetime of experiences—with parents, teachers, bosses, coaches; some helpful, some harmful.

If someone has only known bosses who were dishonest, dismissive, or abusive, why would they expect you to be any different? That's why consistency matters. When team members experience your care, listening, and fairness—day after day—their trust in you grows. And with trust comes openness and engagement. This doesn't happen overnight. Leaders must **earn the right to be listened to and to listen deeply in return**. That means making it safe for employees to share honest input without fear of penalty or dismissal.

3. Organizational Realities

Time and personal histories aside, sometimes **the very structure of an organization** works against good listening. Leaders must actively **create cultures where dissent is not only allowed but welcomed.** Safe spaces for diverse opinions lead to better decisions and greater buy-in.

4. Crisis Management

There are moments when listening must take a back seat—when the kitchen's on fire, or a real emergency demands immediate action. In crisis, we move fast. That's reality. But in these moments, your team's response will reflect the trust and credibility you've built during calmer times. If your past behavior has earned their respect, they'll rally behind your leadership even when you have no time to explain.

5. The Seduction of Being the "Answer Person"

Being asked for advice can feel great. It validates your expertise and authority. But this is dangerous, especially for new managers. Too often, leaders feel they must provide all the answers. In doing so, they rob their teams of growth and engagement. The irony is this: the respect you're chasing is more likely to come when your team sees you **empowering others**, not solving everything yourself.

True empowerment happens when people feel heard and are part of the problem-solving process. It's not about giving answers. It's about asking the right questions and listening deeply.

THE LESSONS:

- **Listening to your people, especially those closest to the front lines—can save you from costly missteps.**
- **Trust earned through consistent listening is your leadership capital in crisis.**
- **Organizations that promote shared decision-making demonstrate authentic respect.**

Questions to Ponder

What obstacles to listening are you most challenged by? What can you do to overcome those obstacles?

Have you ever been surprised by what a team member has told you about work or themselves? Why was it a surprise?

Are your team and leadership hampered by unconstructive talk and complaining? What can you do to improve it?

NOTES

(Your Own Observations)

TERMINATIONS

Our role as leaders and managers is and can be extremely satisfying and pleasing. Unfortunately, we often have a duty to undertake unpleasant jobs. Perhaps the least pleasant one is to terminate one of our staff members. Not a job to be taken lightly. For whatever reason, some hires fail to deliver. My dad used to say that if an employee fails, we either didn't train them well or hired the wrong person. In either case, it is our fault/responsibility. A "Failed" employee may not have the aptitude for the work. They may not have the desire to put themselves "out there" to the guest, or, in a very few cases, they may be averse to doing whatever a person of authority asks of them. In any case, people that fall into this category of not buying into and/or not delivering the critical and vital guest experience must be taken off the team.

Removing someone from the team may involve "Firing" or terminating the person but there are other solutions as well. (See the chapter on "Choices" theory.) With this approach, we embrace the idea that every person is constantly making choices; some are conscious and others are not. Our job, as leaders, is to make sure our staff really understand what choices they are making.

The decision to terminate someone's employment is really the culmination of that employee deciding that either they don't want or can't do the required job. Our job is to be clear about what is the required job, why it is required, and provide an appropriate amount of assistance and training to help the person succeed. If the person fails to deliver, we should make sure we have clarified what choices we have as the leader responsible and what their options are, i.e., to do the job and stay employed, or to try and fail and then resign, or try and fail and have us terminate their employment. In any case, the requirements of the job remain.

Sometimes, the most appropriate solution is to coach them to another industry or job where their skills and desires are better served. The manager of one of our stores had a delightful young team member who loved to visit with the elderly customers. She was great in hospitality, but this restaurant really needed their crew to be hospitable AND speedy. She just could not tear herself away from conversations with the older guests. Our manager suggested to her that a job in food service in a retirement community might be a better fit. She made the choice to look there and found a job that allowed her to make the most of her strengths and desires. Some would say she was fired but she was assisted in making the right choice for her.

Have you ever thought about what emotions are wrapped up in coming to the decision to fire a crew member? Anger, frustration, fear, guilt, concern, and impatience all can come into play. Is it any wonder that we often avoid this dreaded duty, often to the detriment of our remaining crew and ourselves. I have assembled the following list of "Do's and Don'ts" when doing a "termination". These will not make it easy, but my dad always said that if it gets easy, it's time to get out!

DOs and Don'ts of Terminations

1) **DO** the termination in person, not over the phone or through some other person.

2) **DO** spend time preparing and knowing exactly what the thing was that precipitated the termination.

3) **DO** have the exit interview/termination form in front of you when you actually carry out the termination and get it signed then. (See Appendix 3)

4) **DO** state clearly what is happening to the staff member. For example, say, "I am terminating your employment here at Auntie Anne's".

5) **DO** stay calm during the interview. Be prepared to be quiet and listen.

6) **DO** be truthful in your reasons for termination.

7) **DO** be non-discriminatory and fair in determination of a termination.

8) **DO** allow the employee to vent their frustrations and record their feelings on the exit interview. Often having the chance to just write out their feelings is enough to avoid a contest over the fairness of the termination.

9) **DO NOT** take anything the employee says personally. Be prepared for them to say awful things about and to you. Remain calm and know that it is a normal reaction to being "rejected" by a boss.

10) **DO NOT** terminate an employee in the heat of battle. If a person does something to make you scream, send them home and tell them they will have to come to speak to you at another time. You may terminate them then, but you will do a more professional job and avoid lawsuits.

11) **DO NOT** allow a Shift Leader or Shift Supervisor to terminate someone. They always have the prerogative of sending a person home and requiring them to meet with you and the SL/SS at your convenience before they will work again.

12) **DO NOT** terminate for theft unless you catch someone with their hand in the till or giving food or cash over the counter. We do terminate people for failing to follow proper cash handling procedures, or for being inaccurate on the till and in cash

handling. Accusing someone of theft is a serious charge and requires clear, unadulterated proof with witnesses to the crime.

13) **DO** attempt to salvage an employee before termination is required.

Salvaging may involve changes in schedule, a change in job responsibilities, or a transfer to another store (do not just transfer your problems, however!). A clear performance review that is brutally frank and candidly honest can salvage an employee. Often a person will decide to leave when they see they are not fit for these positions. Waiting for them to quit or to be terminated leaves their exit in an uncontrolled situation. Often a person will acknowledge their performance shortcomings and change their behavior. How cool is that?!

There is research that indicates about eighty percent terminated employees are much happier in their next job. That should provide some relief to a manager who struggles over this part of their job. Terminations are not fun. We do fewer of them as the labor market gets tighter and tighter. Unfortunately, they are still required, and it is the manager's job to carry it out in a way that is legal, avoids ongoing hassles, and allows the person the most dignity in leaving.

If you have questions or concerns about a termination or anticipate an employee who is quickly moving down the road toward being fired, contact your supervisor, the HR department, or a valued mentor for advice.

Sometimes the Result is Better for Everyone Even When It Results in Termination

A FRONT LINE TALE

Connie was in high school when she came to work for us as a part-time crew person. She graduated, moved into a Team Leader position and eventually an Assistant Manager role. The time came to fill the Manager position in a store where she had worked very successfully as a "Number Two". We made the offer, and she accepted enthusiastically. It would have been hard to find a team member whom the guests loved more than Connie. Her crew liked her but more as a friend than as a manager. That is not all bad unless or until those friendships stand in the way of managing the store to the standards of the company and the rest of the organization.

Connie also had challenges with meeting deadlines and following up. We sent her to time-management workshops, and seminars for the first-time supervisor, and coached her extensively. Our company's system required meetings over performance and discipline always to be followed up with a letter that described the meeting, any conclusions made, and any consequences that would result from either failure or a success.

This was the case with Connie. Unfortunately, we concluded that a change in management was necessary. I came to the store early one morning when she was getting ready to open. I had told her I would be coming and had to talk to her. When I entered the store, she looked up at me and said "This is it, isn't it? You're going to let me go."

I told her that was correct, and she started to cry and tell me she totally understood, and this had been the best job she had ever had. She loved the company and hoped I "wouldn't hate her". She was not angry. In some ways, I think she was relieved. To this day we remain friends.

She has gotten married (I was invited to the wedding), has had two children, and a fabulous family.

THE LESSONS:

- **Recognize that terminations do have to occur.**
- **There is a right way and many wrong ways to do them.**
- **Sometimes there is a solution that truly is a "Win-Win" available.**
- **People being terminated should have an idea that it is coming. This means expectations and coaching must be clear and consequences spelled out. (See Corrective Action in the Personnel Action Form, in Appendix 2)**

Questions to Ponder

Do you view terminations as something to avoid at all costs?

Do you look forward to terminations?

How can you avoid taking things personally?

NOTES

(Your Own Observations)

KURT SCHAUERMANN

NOT ALL STORIES END WELL

Sometimes an addiction is so powerful that no amount of employer engagement or sincere listening can overcome it. We've found that methamphetamine is often one of those addictions. This was certainly the case with a young man we had brought along as a Team Leader at one of our Seattle stores. Despite our best intentions, countless heartfelt conversations, and a deep investment in time and coaching, Bill would not face his addiction or the toll it took on himself, his future, and his job. The breaking point came when he admitted to "borrowing" funds from the till. We had to let him go.

Another story—not coincidentally also involving meth—was a young man trying to reclaim his life after treatment. He was the son of a manager and incredibly talented. But he, too, could not stay clean. Eventually, he took over $7,000 in cash deposits and vanished. To this day, I don't know if he is alive or dead. It is heartbreaking.

The Case for "Directed Rage

Many of the stories shared here seem to say that if you listen well, fully engage your staff, and are a great manager, all will be well and running a business will just flow easily. To those of you who have been in business for some time, you know that is not the truth. What really happens is that our people sometimes fail. Sometimes the best intentions go awry. Sometimes a person just drops the ball, and the consequences can be very serious.

Every manager has a different style, and my style is to be generally pretty good-natured. I rarely raise my voice and almost never express anger. This was not always the case. Many of us have worked with or around managers who are constantly in crisis mode. They may be angry a good share of the time or even resort to regular spats of loud voices. Often, we begin to "tune out" these managers because their anger is the norm, not the exception.

Our operations person shared with me an unexpected incident that triggered his anger when he *went into one of our stores and, looking at the walk-in refrigerator, saw* an intolerable condition. He confessed he did not, like normal, ask the manager how her family was and what the latest was with her grandchildren. He "exploded" and told her that what he saw was totally unacceptable and that he was close to not having the store open that day until it was corrected.

He was mad. She had violated the trust he had placed in her and it was inexcusable in his mind. I call this kind of reaction "Righteous Anger" or "Directed Rage". He was right to have this kind of reaction. It was very effective at both motivating the manager to get it corrected and, I expect, not to let it happen again. It was out of the norm for this operations person to react like this. I am very confident that the manager was not offended but more embarrassed by the circumstances.

This Vice-President of Operations had earned the right to be heard and to react this way because of the way he had interacted in the past. If this was a normal response by the operations lead to shortcomings in the store, it probably would not have been as effective or as accepted.

THE LESSONS:

- **Stories of employees overcoming the odds are inspiring—and we need them. But not all stories end that way. When our efforts to help do not lead to a happy ending, we can't let that stop us. We are still called to be a positive influence, to invest, to care. Even when it does not work out, it matters that we tried.**

- **Reacting honestly to an unacceptable situation is both good management as well as effective at changing behavior IF it is not the common way a supervisor interacts with their team.**
- **Righteous anger is Righteous!**

Questions to Ponder

Does having a "Not good result" event cause you to withdraw and hold back investing in your people?

Do you overuse the anger approach to management? Do you under-use it?

In your business, what would be a cause of Righteous Anger?

NOTES

(Your Own Observations)

Listening to the Dissenting Voice

I was reminded recently of the movie *Big*, starring Tom Hanks. In it, a young boy magically becomes an adult overnight and finds himself working as a marketing executive at a toy company. In one memorable scene, the executive team is gathered to hear a pitch for a new toy. While the others nod along, Tom Hanks's character—Josh, a 12-year-old in a grown man's body—raises his hand and says, "*I don't get it.*"

The CEO pauses and asks him to elaborate. Josh picks up the toy, fiddles with it, breaks it, and then repeats: "*It's not fun.*" While the presenter is visibly irritated and embarrassed, the CEO listens carefully and says, "*I understand. You're right.*"

What struck me about that scene is how rare it is for leaders to pause and actually listen to the dissenting voice—especially when that voice is timid, unfamiliar, or not part of the usual power structure. But when we do, better decisions often follow.

I witnessed a real-life version of this during a Franchisee Advisory Council meeting I attended. These sessions brought together 15–18 operators from around the country for long presentations from the corporate team, covering everything from marketing to operations to technology.

At one meeting, the corporate staff were promoting a new technology platform. But they were doing it in the usual way—top-down, with slides and speeches. There was an obvious lack of enthusiasm from the franchisees in the room, but no one said anything. The corporate team, unaware or unwilling to read the room, kept pushing.

As I sat there, it became clear to me that I wasn't going to embrace this technology for some very specific reasons. But rather than simply speaking up for myself, I wanted to know what the other franchisees were really thinking. I asked that we stop the presentation and go around the room, one by one, so every operator could share their honest opinion.

What came out of that conversation was powerful: almost every operator at the table said they would not support the new technology. Not because they didn't believe in innovation—but because their trust in the corporation's ability to *execute* was gone. Past rollouts had been poorly handled, and no one believed this one would be different.

The corporate team was clearly uncomfortable. But to his credit, the CEO approached me after the meeting and said, *"That was the most important conversation we've had in a Council meeting."*

Within a month, they backed off the initiative and restructured their entire approach to technology. But it took too long—and too much effort—for those voices to be heard in the first place.

In both the movie and the real-world example, meaningful change happened only when the leader was willing to pause, listen to the quiet or dissenting voice, and *truly hear* what was being said.

THE LESSONS:

- **Great leaders don't just listen to the loudest voices—they actively seek out the quiet ones.**
- **When team members feel safe enough to speak candidly, it can reveal blind spots that change the course of decisions for the better.**
- **Trust is the currency that gives people the courage to speak honestly. Leaders must earn it, nurture it, and protect it, especially when uncomfortable truths surface.**
- **This trust can result in unique and valuable perspectives that may turn the organization away from a poor move or, at the very least, improve the product.**

Questions to Ponder

Are there dissenting voices that have become silenced over time? Is that a result of them not really being listened to?

In meetings, who is the first to speak? Is it the leader (maybe you!) or does your team feel comfortable expressing opinions that may be contrary to yours?

NOTES

(Your Own Observations)

CHANGE IS GOOD? CHANGE IS BAD?

Just when I think I've seen it all, something reminds me how different we all are, especially when it comes to change. Recently, I was reminded that **everyone reacts to change differently.**

For some, it's energizing. For others, it's unsettling.

Two Very Different Responses to Change

1. The "Change Lovers"

Some people *thrive* on change. They get excited by trying new things—switching up routines, and finding creative ways to make improvements.

I remember one manager at Centerfoods who couldn't go more than six months without rearranging the back room. He wasn't doing it efficiently, he just needed something *different.* His energy and appetite for the new made him a great person to experiment with. But for his crew? It was exhausting. They wanted predictability.

How to lead them:

- Feed their appetite for variety with special projects and creative challenges.
- Don't expect them to love a long-term routine.
- Use their adaptability to pilot new initiatives—but give the team some breathing room from constant change.

2. The "Routine Seekers"

On the other end of the spectrum are those who *crave consistency.* These are the people who like to start at the same time every day, follow a clear process, and execute with precision.

Rich was a long-time manager for our company. He seemed so resistant to change it drove me nuts. I would come into his store and suggest some changes and all I heard was why it wouldn't work or how it was not a good approach. Sometimes the changes were mandated by our franchiser. We had little choice but to make the change. I knew that if Rich wouldn't buy into it, it would not last. Finally, I tried, at the suggestion of a counselor I was seeing, to give him time to absorb the change idea and think about how he might implement it. No deadlines but I did give him a chance to sleep on it, think about it and to consider the uniqueness of his store. It was amazing how he would eventually both accept the change and own its implementation. He just needed time to figure out how he was going to make it a routine.

When change is needed, routine seekers may seem resistant. But here is what I've earned: **they're not refusing—they're processing.** And once they have had time to understand the why and how, they are often the best at making change stick.

How to lead them:

- Give them time to reflect and ask questions.
- Let them own the implementation process.
- Set clear deadlines and expectations—but don't rush the "buy-in" process.
- Once they're on board, you'll see strong, steady execution.

Finding the Balance

Every team is made up of people across the "change continuum." As a manager, it's your job to recognize where each person fits and adapt your approach accordingly. You'll not only get better results—you will also increase satisfaction and engagement.

THE LESSONS:

- **Resistance to change isn't always resistance—it might just be a different style of adapting.**
- **Some people love change. Others need time to embrace it.**
- **As a leader, flex your approach and make the most of each team member's strengths.**

Questions to Ponder

Who are the change lovers? Who are the routine lovers?

What are obstacles you face when implementing change in your organization?

NOTES

(Your Own Observations)

BUILDING A TEAM—THE LEADER'S ROLE

We do not talk enough about the critical role leaders—and their Assistants, Shift Supervisors, and Shift Leaders—play in building a formidable team. It is no exaggeration to say that every conversation a leader has either builds up the team or tears it down.

Leaders build teams by teaching, training, offering constructive feedback, recognizing excellent work, encouraging effort, and fostering a motivating environment. On the other hand, they tear teams down through gossip, public criticism, and any form of harassment or discrimination. Equally harmful is remaining silent or complicit when these behaviors occur.

So, what should a Team Leader do when they witness another leader tearing down the team through gossip or negativity? As difficult as it may be, they must speak up. Leadership requires rejecting passivity and standing up for a culture of respect and teamwork. This may involve confronting the offending leader directly, enlisting a higher-level supervisor to help address the issue, or facilitating a solution-oriented discussion within the leadership team.

To be clear, this is not an endorsement of ignoring inferior performance. Addressing performance issues is a vital part of leadership—but it must be done constructively and directly with the person involved. Leaders may need to collaborate to develop a plan for improvement, but it should always be focused on solutions, not venting or back-channel complaints.

THE LESSONS:

- **Listening isn't always easy—but it is always essential. Despite the very real obstacles, there is no substitute for listening as a tool to build trust, loyalty, and excellence.**
- **When you ask good questions—and truly listen—your people will give you insights you might never uncover otherwise.**
- **Understanding why your team stays and performs well can help you define the non-negotiables in your culture.**
- **Transitioning from manager to leader means shifting your focus from just the work to the people doing the work—and understanding what matters most to them.**
- **The time to listen is when you don't have time for it!**
- **Really hearing your team members takes practice and intention.**
- **Excellent execution requires trust; trust built through good listening in the past.**
- **Engagement and Connection are beneficial to all the stakeholders.**

Questions to Ponder

What is your biggest obstacle to really listening to your team?

Have you ever been surprised by what a team member has told you about work or themselves?

Why was it a surprise?

Is your team and leadership hampered by unconstructive talk and complaining?

What can you do to improve it?

NOTES

(Your Own Observations)

PART 3

ENGAGEMENT

LISTENING

Earning the Right to Be Heard—By Listening First

Every employee brings with them a lifetime of experiences—some good, some difficult. They are shaped by parents, teachers, coaches, bosses, and mentors. If those past figures were inconsistent, absent, manipulative, or abusive, it's likely they'll approach their current leaders with skepticism or guardedness.

But here is the good news:

Consistent care, listening, and mentoring from you can rewrite someone's entire story. We must earn the right to speak into someone's life—not just by having the title, but by listening first, showing care, and being present.

Real Impact Does Not Come Overnight

People often ask how we have retained managers so long—our average tenure is over eighteen years, which is almost unheard of in our industry. I do not believe we have a secret formula, other than this:

We treat each manager as a whole person, not just another asset to manage. We see their *stories*, their *struggles*, and their *dreams*. We listen. We invest.

It amazes me how some leaders refer to their teams like numbers on a spreadsheet. That mindset misses the human element entirely—and it is the human element that builds real loyalty and real growth.

HOW TO MOTIVATE? THAT'S *NOT* THE QUESTION

One of the most common questions I hear is:

"Kurt, how do we motivate our crews to sell better? Show up on time? Deliver better customer service?"

That's a tall order. And honestly, it's the wrong question.

At a recent seminar, I was introduced to a better way to look at it. What if we stopped trying to *motivate* people and instead focused on creating *an environment where people can motivate themselves?*

Because the truth is—motivation has to come from within. Our job as leaders is to create the conditions that allow it to thrive.

What does a self-motivating environment look like?

Here's a simple framework. Ask yourself—and then your team—these questions. And listen closely to the answers:

1. **Am I listened to?** Does my opinion matter?
2. **Is my work meaningful?** Would anyone notice if I wasn't here? Do I make a difference?
3. **Is it fun to work here?** Do I enjoy my coworkers? Is my boss fair, approachable, even fun?
4. **Am I paid fairly?** Compared to others doing the same kind of work, am I compensated appropriately?
5. **Does this place have high standards?** Am I proud to tell people where I work?

6. **Am I appreciated?** When I do a great job, does anyone notice or say thank you?
7. **Do my values align with this job?** Am I ever asked to do something that feels wrong to me?

These are not abstract questions. They are the *core drivers* of engagement and personal investment.

So instead of asking "How do I motivate my people?"

Ask:

- What might be demotivating them right now?
- Have I created an environment where people want to do great work?

How Much Do Your Team Members Really Know?

(Tailored to the Food Service Industry—but applicable in any business)

Let's ask a few key questions:

- Do your team members know what your sales were last week?
- Do they know if sales are trending up or down this month or year?
- Do *crew members*, not just shift leaders, know what your target **Sales per Man-Hour (CPMH)** is? Do they even know how it's calculated?
- What about your **Cost of Goods Sold (COGS)** last month? Was it better or worse than usual?
- Do they understand the difference between *sales* and *profit?*
- Do they know what your **average check** is? What the goal is? How you're trending?

Sharing this kind of business information might feel risky—but in our company, it's been one of the most powerful ways to build a true *team.*

I believe in the value of every team member, from the newest counter person to the most seasoned supervisor. Their contribution starts with great service and quality work—but when they're trusted with meaningful business info, their *ownership* of the store's success takes a huge leap forward.

Each store is like its own engine. And for that engine to run smoothly, every cylinder has to be firing. **One of the biggest drivers of performance? Crew motivation.** And motivation skyrockets when people understand the goals—and know they're trusted to help achieve them.

Feel Alone in Your Store?

If you feel like you're the only one carrying the weight, maybe it's time to *recruit your own crew as your team of assistants.* That means involving them in the bigger picture:

- Share specifics—sales growth, CPMH targets, average check goals, shopper scores.
- Teach them to calculate performance metrics during the shift.
- Ask them to track customer counts, check sizes, or daily sales comparisons to last year.
- Call in and ask for updates—what's our sales growth today? What was customer count last hour?

These conversations spark engagement and awareness. And they signal something important:

"You matter. You're a part of this."

There's simply too much ground to cover for one manager to carry the full load. Building a strong business means *building a strong team*—and that starts with sharing the "why" behind the work.

THE LESSONS:

When a team—or even just one individual—seems unmotivated, check the temperature. Ask questions, listen, adjust.

- **If someone clearly isn't aligned with the work or the expectations, move them off the team. Mismatched people will drag down even the best culture.**
- **If the whole team feels off, don't lecture—ask. Find out what they need to re-engage, then work to build the environment where excellence is the natural result.**
- **If you don't share information, your team will fill the void with their own assumptions.**
- **Teaching your people about key business metrics gives them more than a job—it gives them ownership.**
- **Your frontline team members aren't just doers—they can be drivers of your success. Start recruiting them as partners today.**

Questions to Ponder

What specifically can you do to improve the atmosphere of motivation in your business?

How much do your subordinates really know about your business?

Do you know what assumptions your people have already made about your business? How profitable it is? How much you make on each sale? What it cost you to build out your business, financially?

NOTES

(Your Own Observations)

UNLEASHING ORGANIZATIONAL POWER

A FRONT LINE TALE

Tom James was a breakfast cook at one of our full-service restaurants. Hardworking and reliable, he quickly became a valued part of the team. But Tom stood out for another reason—his mouth and face were severely distorted, making it difficult for him to speak clearly. One day, we sat down to talk, and I asked him about it. That's when Tom shared his story.

He was born in Florida and, at one point, had been living in a garbage dumpster. Eventually, he made his way to Seattle in search of a better life, hoping to reconnect with a brother who lived there. But his past followed him—Tom struggled with drug addiction and found himself facing a choice between jail and rehab. He chose rehab, which fortunately included stable housing.

As an infant, Tom had suffered an infection that affected the development of his jaw. While in rehab, he began receiving medical care and underwent the first of what was supposed to be a series of corrective surgeries. However, once he got a job and was no longer eligible for state-funded healthcare, his access to treatment stopped. His new health insurance wouldn't cover the remaining procedures due to pre-existing condition exclusions. He was caught in a classic "Catch-22."

Tom eventually became a Kitchen Manager with us, earning everyone's respect through his commitment and reliability. Moved by his story, I started asking questions about what it would take to complete his medical journey. The next surgery was scheduled at the University of Washington and estimated to cost around $14,000. Tom would also need about four weeks off work to recover.

We decided to do something about it.

We created what we called a **"Family Fund."** It wasn't a formal nonprofit or company initiative, just a simple way for us to pool resources to help Tom. We reached out to our vendors, partners, and eventually our own employees to see if they wanted to contribute. The response was overwhelming. In just three months, we had raised more than enough to cover the surgery and Tom's time off.

We also contacted the hospital and medical team to see if anyone would consider donating their services. While the hospital couldn't help, the surgeon agreed to donate his fee. The anesthesiologist couldn't, but between the donations and the discounts, we made it happen.

Tom had the surgery—and eight months later, the final procedure. The transformation was astonishing. The young man who once avoided eye contact now carried himself with confidence. The difference wasn't just physical—it was emotional and psychological. Today, Tom is married and has two beautiful daughters. He's a blessing to his family and his community.

What started as a one-time act of support didn't stop there. The Family Fund continued for more than fifteen years. Over that time, it provided **over $150,000** in support—through outright grants and no-interest loans—for a wide variety of employee needs:

- Helping a young woman rebuild her life after a fire destroyed her apartment.
- Covering uninsured medical expenses.
- Funding car repairs, tuition, or emergency travel—like flying a woman to Texas to retrieve her children from an abusive situation.

Amazingly, the default rate on those no-interest loans was less than one percent.

But the most powerful outcome wasn't financial—it was cultural. The sense of community, trust, and belonging that grew among our team was transformative. People showed up for one another in ways that went far beyond the job. It built a team, and it built a family.

THE LESSONS:

- **Listening—really listening—can uncover life-changing opportunities to lead and support.**
- **When leaders invite their teams to rally around something meaningful, they spark a deep sense of community.**
- **A strong culture of care can turn a workplace into something much more: a source of strength, resilience, and shared purpose.**

Questions to Ponder

Are there areas that your team would benefit from joining together to tackle?

NOTES

(Your Own Observations)

"IT TAKES TWO TO TANGO!"

As leaders, we often strive to build a positive work environment—one grounded in respect, open communication, and mutual understanding. But even with the best intentions and a genuine commitment to listening, sometimes things don't go as planned. Why? Because despite good listening, it takes two to tango.

A FRONT LINE TALE

Cheryl was one of the first employees we hired. She began as a part-time counter person at a quick-serve pie shop we operated. Over time, she earned promotions and transitioned into new roles—not always because her skills matched the job, but often out of appreciation for her loyalty. Eventually, she landed in an administrative position where she controlled the flow of information throughout the company. Internally, we started calling her "The Keeper of the Keys."

While this role gave her a sense of importance, it became a problem. Cheryl began withholding key information—intentionally or not—as a way to maintain control. For her, it was a security blanket. For the rest of the team, it was an obstacle that caused ongoing frustration and breakdowns in workflow.

We had numerous meetings—well-documented and respectfully conducted—where I addressed the issue directly. I asked Cheryl for her thoughts on solving the problems. I asked if she could make specific changes in how she communicated. Her response, time and time again, was that *everyone* else needed to change. She took no responsibility. She never acknowledged the real impact of her behavior.

Eventually, I gave her two options:

1. Accept a different role with fewer responsibilities, a reduced schedule, and a pay adjustment.
2. Take a generous severance package and transition out of the company.

I put everything in writing. I gave her time to think it over. I made it clear that if no choice was made, I would have to make it for her.

When the deadline arrived, Cheryl simply said, "You're not going to fire me."

I handed her the prepared termination letter, outlining the severance package and final details. She stood in shock. Despite all the conversations, despite the clear choices, despite the time and space to consider them, she hadn't listened. Or perhaps, she just couldn't *hear* what was being said.

This experience reminded me that some people wrap their identity so tightly around their job that they lose perspective. Their sense of self-worth is tethered to their role. And when that role is challenged, they cling even harder—often to their own detriment and that of the organization.

The good news is Cheryl found a new position at another company where her attention to detail was a perfect fit. She stayed there for over fifteen years. She just needed a different environment—one better suited to her needs and strengths.

THE POWER OF A SMALL CONVERSATION

A FRONT LINE TALE

A young man named Steve once worked for us. He did not have his high school diploma, and at one dinner with another manager, he shared how much that weighed on him. I made an offhand comment:

"You are too smart to not get that done.
You are your own worst enemy. Just do it."

Eight years later, Steve earned his **GED**, went on to **college**, got a **Bachelor's degree in Communications**, and eventually went back to his high school to request his real diploma—something offered to GED recipients who complete a university degree. He said it was one of his proudest moments. That one sentence stuck with him for nearly a decade.

Mentorship That Lasts a Lifetime

During that same period, Steve and I had regular breakfasts. We talked about life, work, and family. One day he shared about his daughter. He wasn't married to her mother, but was committed to being present. I shared something simple that stuck with me from research I had read:

"The quality of a girl's adult relationships is most often tied to the quality of her relationship with her father."

Years later, Steve told me that piece of advice changed how he showed up as a dad. It helped guide his decisions and prioritize his presence.

Update on Steve

Today, Steve is the **Vice President of Operations** for a 20-location chain including **Auntie Anne's Pretzels, Cinnabon**, and **Starbuck's**. His daughter? She is now **a college graduate, happily married, and a new mother.**

Who would have thought that a few shared meals and intentional listening would echo twenty years down the road?

You never know what kind of legacy you are building just by sitting, listening, and *really seeing someone.*

THE LESSONS:

- **Listening is not just a management skill—it's a leadership superpower.**
- **You don't earn influence by talking. You earn it by being there—consistently.**
- **People remember the small moments more than you realize.**
- **Invest in others like their story depends on it—because sometimes, it does.**

Questions to Ponder

How can you improve your listening skills?

Who might benefit from your improved listening skills?

NOTES

(Your Own Observations)

TAKING CARE OF CUSTOMERS

Everyone's Role

"If we're not taking care of guests right now, nothing else matters."

In our business, guest care isn't just *someone's* job—it's *everyone's* job. One of the mos powerful truths in service is this:

If the crew isn't taking care of the guests right *now*, it doesn't matter what the plan is for an hour from now, the next shift, or next year.

But it works both ways.

If leadership isn't making sure we can take care of guests next year, there won't be any guests to serve next month, next week, or even tomorrow.

This mutual dependence is the heart of a strong business. Each level of leadership supports the level below—and relies on the level above. No one role is more important; every role is essential.

The Guest Care Ladder

Here's how the responsibility for customer care scales across the organization:

Crew Person's Role

Take care of the guests *right now*, and prepare for those arriving *shortly.*

Team Leader's Role

All of the above, **plus** focus on taking care of guests in the *next hour* and *next shift.*

Team Supervisor/Assistant Manager's Role

All of the above, **plus** focus on guests *tomorrow* and in the *next few days.*

General Manager's Role

All of the above, **plus** ensure we're ready to serve guests *next week* and *next month.*

Senior General Manager's Role

All of the above, **plus** plan and act for guests *next month* and *six months* from now.

Vice President's Role

All of the above, **plus** ensure we can take care of guests *six months* from now and in the *coming year.*

Owner / President's Role

All of the above, **plus** do the work now that guarantees we'll be able to serve guests *next year* and *five years* from now.

Leadership Starts with Presence

I often walk into a location and, if a guest needs help, I jump in. Not because it's my "job"—but because it sends a message. *Every guest matters.* If I walk past that guest, I'm silently telling the team that guest care isn't really our top priority.

But when I stop and help, I'm modeling exactly what matters most: **Serving the guest now is the priority of every person in every role.**

YOUR Turn:

What are the **vital, front-line duties** in your role or business—those that, if neglected, cause everything else to crumble?

THE LESSONS:

- **Make sure everyone on your team understands their role in achieving *outstanding guest care*, and how they fit into the big picture. We're all in this together—and *every rung on the ladder matters.***

Questions to Ponder

If you asked any person on your team what their priority is, would they answer "taking care of our customers"?

What are the vital front line duties and priorities for your business?

NOTES

(Your Own Observations)

TAKING CARE OF EACH OTHER

Good Listening Can Result in Unorthodox but Positive Solutions

Larry was hired as an area supervisor and brought with him a wealth of experience from working with another restaurant chain in a different part of the country. For the first year or so, things went well. But after about two years, the wheels started coming off.

We couldn't keep managers in the stores Larry was overseeing, and he was logging ridiculous hours trying to hold everything together. It became clear something wasn't right.

Larry was married and had two kids about the same age as mine. We had several coaching sessions—and a few "Come to Jesus" meetings. Eventually, he opened and shared that his marriage was falling apart. He was deeply involved in a difficult custody battle and juggling the demands of parenting while trying to perform at a high level professionally. He told me he was committed to improving, and we gave it a few more months. But things didn't improve. Finally, I called him in for a meeting.

He knew what was coming—or so I thought.

When Larry walked into the office, he asked if he could speak before I said anything. I said, "Go ahead."

What followed completely changed the trajectory of the conversation.

He acknowledged, upfront, that I had every right to fire him. He owned the fact that he hadn't delivered, and he didn't make excuses. But then he offered something unexpected: a solution.

He proposed that instead of letting him go, we would allow him to take over management of one of our smaller stores—one that had been notoriously difficult to staff. It was one of the stores in his district, so he knew the challenges well. He said, "Let me manage that location. Pay me less than I'm making now—something between a store manager and a supervisor. It won't require a district manager, and I believe I can stabilize it."

He explained that running one store would give him the structure and predictability he needed to care for his children, manage school pickups and drop-offs, and work through the final stages of his divorce. "If it doesn't work, you can let me go," he added.

I told him I'd think about it and get back to him the next day. That night, I considered everything carefully. I also reached out to a few trusted peers, some of whom advised against it. "These arrangements rarely work," they said.

But after some reflection, prayer, and a firm outline of what I'd need to see from him, I decided to take a chance.

And I'm glad I did.

Larry took over the store—and it flourished. In the two and a half years he managed it, we made more money than that location had ever generated before. He honored every part of our agreement, and the situation turned into a win-win-win: for the business, for Larry, and for his kids.

Today, Larry is managing a nonprofit organization that employs people with disabilities.

He's thriving—and so are the people he serves.

THE LESSONS:

- **A leader is always doing one of two things, building up or tearing down. Which one are you doing? Talking *to* people, not *about* them, is a mark of strong leadership. Gossip and indirect criticism are destructive to the health of any team.**
- **Be open to creative, unorthodox solutions, especially when they come from those closest to the problem.**
- **Listen with empathy, not just authority. People will often surprise you with their honesty and ingenuity.**
- **Set clear expectations, but don't be afraid to lead with humanity. The payoff can be powerful—for everyone involved.**

Questions to Ponder

Identify one characteristic, either you have seen or know about yourself, that has a tendency to tear down the team.

Have you considered unorthodox solutions to management challenges?

What characteristics are necessary for an unorthodox solution to work?

NOTES

(Your Own Observations)

Replacing Valued Veterans in the Restaurant Business (and Similar Environments)

At some point, every manager finds themselves facing a wave of turnover, especially of key, veteran team members. Whether it's part of the natural ebb and flow of the industry or the growing pains of a new leadership transition, there are times when it feels like all the experienced people are leaving at once. Suddenly, you are surrounded by rookies and are trying to keep things running smoothly.

Let us be honest, many of us have come to rely on those veterans. Their initiative, their ability to anticipate needs, and their calming presence during chaos made our jobs easier. When they are gone, it can feel overwhelming.

We will talk about how to avoid losing those great people, but here, let's focus on what to do when you're in the middle of this difficult transition.

So, How Do You Rebuild It?

First, understand what made those veterans so valuable in the first place. Yes, time on the job helped. But more importantly, they were **given the skills and permission to take initiative.**

They did not just "become good"—they were *developed.*

Ask your Team Leaders how they got their role, and you will often hear:

- "I was the best at my job."
- "I asked for the opportunity."
- "My manager encouraged me."

What you will not often hear is:

- "I was recognized for my initiative."

And that's part of the problem. Many managers fail to explicitly acknowledge why someone stood out, and what behavior earned them more responsibility. If we aren't naming what we value, how can others learn to replicate it?

What to Look For in Your Future Veterans

To build up the next generation of leaders, start by identifying the core traits of a strong veteran:

1. **Competence** – They can perform at a high level, with speed and accuracy.
2. **Trust** – You can rely on them to work independently and they have good character.
3. **Example-setting** – Their behavior positively influences the rest of the team.
4. **Team Impact** – Their presence improves flow, morale, and productivity.

But here's the catch—promoting someone is not the end of the journey. In fact, it's just the beginning.

Too often, we see newly promoted leaders lose their edge:

- They get stuck behind a desk doing paperwork.
- They stay too busy with tasks instead of leading the team.
- They try to "save labor" by working short-handed, doing all the work themselves.

These habits undermine their impact as leaders.

What's the Fix?

Start by stepping back and observing. Literally. **Stand back and watch them work.** Then, **pull them off the floor** and talk about what you both saw.

Ask simple, powerful questions:

- "What do you see happening out there?"
- "What do you think went well?"
- "What would you have done differently?"

This shifts their mindset from *worker bee* to *leader.* You're training their eyes to see the bigger picture—just like yours. And do it regularly. Not just on slow afternoons, but during the pressure of a Saturday rush. **Make time to coach.** Stop in unexpectedly. Show up for the close. Be present.

Use the EDOCA Method:

- **Explain** – Tell them what success looks like.
- **Demonstrate** – Show them what you mean.
- **Observe** – Let them try it, and watch.
- **Coach** – Offer real-time feedback.
- **Assess** – Evaluate how they're growing.

When you feel like it is "impossible to replace a great veteran," chances are it's just a gap in development—not talent.

THE LESSONS:

- **Leaders aren't born. They're built.**
- **Developing someone starts with setting clear expectations.**
- **Observing and coaching outside the normal workflow gives both of you fresh perspective.**
- **EDOCA (Explain, Demonstrate, Observe, Coach, Assess) is a simple, powerful framework for growth.**
- ***Bonus tip:* Recognize your leaders—not just with words, but with compensation. If they're doing more, acknowledge it. That's how you retain them longer.**

Questions to Ponder

Who might be flying under your radar that has the basic characteristics for being a leader?

If your best current leader/veteran leaves, who would you consider as the "next batter up"?

Is your tendency to rely on your veterans standing in the way of you developing the next one? How can you adjust that?

NOTES

(Your Own Observations)

A Law Firm Story

In 2015, I was asked to help my brother's law firm navigate a significant transition. My brother, who had served as the Managing Director since the firm's founding, was preparing to retire. The firm has been highly successful, and they had recently brought in two young attorneys as partners to help carry the business into its next chapter. The goal was to shift leadership responsibilities from my brother and his longtime partner (who was also nearing retirement) to the new generation.

In a personal injury law firm, much of the success hinges on the support staff—paralegals, typists, receptionists, and office managers. These team members ensure deadlines are met, clients are treated with care, and new cases are smoothly onboard. My brother's firm had excelled at hiring, training, and retaining high-performing people in these roles. Staff turnover was rare, and morale was high.

The partners met several times a year to review cases and discuss personnel matters, including compensation. One partner conducted regular one-on-one check-ins with the staff to understand how they were doing and to surface any concerns. These insights were shared at partner meetings.

With the leadership transition underway, I encouraged the partner conducting these interviews to shift his focus slightly. I asked him to dig deeper—to understand **why** the team had stayed so loyal, what had driven their performance, and what values had made the firm feel like home. This was not just about managing change; it was about identifying the cultural ingredients that made the firm successful so they could be preserved going forward.

At first, the interviewing partner was skeptical. He worried the questions I suggested would feel too personal or difficult for staff to answer. But he was in for a surprise.

Here are a few of the key questions we included:

1. **Why do you work here, as opposed to another law firm?**
2. **What would make you consider leaving? What changes would give you second thoughts about staying?**
3. **How is this firm different from the others you've worked at?**
4. **What values does this firm stand for?**
5. **With Craig's (my brother's) retirement approaching, what are your concerns?**

There were a few other questions, but these five were the heart of the conversation.

When the partner reported back at the next partner meeting, the results stunned everyone. The two younger attorneys were deeply impacted. Until then, they had been entirely focused on the legal work—the cases, the court dates, the outcomes. But the interviews opened their eyes to something bigger: **the responsibility of leadership** is not just **managing cases—it's nurturing culture.**

Some of the most insightful responses from staff included:

- *"I work here because they share the firm's success. When we win big, we are rewarded—and they do not keep secrets."*
- *"The attorneys don't ask me to lie to their wives."*
- *"They really care about the clients—no matter what they look like or how they talk."*
- *"This office is about business, not partying or drama."*

These answers were not just heartening, they were revealing. The firm's culture was built on **trust, transparency, integrity, and mutual respect.** And it was working.

The partner who conducted the interviews had built strong relationships with the staff over time. He had earned their trust—and therefore, their honesty. The younger attorneys took what they heard to heart. They embraced the values described and made a clear decision to **lead with the same principles.**

Now, a decade after my brother's retirement, the firm is thriving. They have added attorneys and support staff, but remarkably, the original core team remains intact. Turnover is still incredibly low, and the culture has remained strong.

THE LESSONS:

- **When you ask good questions—and truly listen—your people will give you insights you might never uncover otherwise.**
- **Understanding why your team stays and performs well can help you define the non-negotiables in your culture.**

- **Transitioning from manager to leader means shifting your focus from just the work to the people doing the work—and understanding what matters most to them.**

WHY WE DO WHAT WE DO

We Measure Success with More Than Numbers and Profits

It sometimes gets lost on us that we are more than a business in the business to make money. Certainly, we must be profitable to stay in business but…there is much more to it for my wife and me. Relationships with our team members, managers, guests and vendors are perhaps most important. Our company mantra "Good People Who Care" has been in place for more than forty years. We take it seriously. I learned some lessons the hard way. I have ignored our responsibility to our teams in the short run to make money. In the long run it cost me both self-esteem, money, and the respect of the very people I care most about. I am committed to not let that happen again. When I say our Good People, I mean ALL OUR PEOPLE. Not just managers but also those crew members who make our lives and the lives of our guests better.

The ultimate measure of our success is the stories of the people whose lives we have touched. Are we thought of as good and fair bosses? Are we spoken of as people who added value to the lives of the people we are charged with leading? When people think of working at Centerfoods, do they see it as a place where they learned valuable life lessons? Would they recommend us as an employer to their friends or, better yet, their children?

How will your team members talk about you in the future? Will you be a "Plus" in their lives, or a "Minus"? I challenge you to think and act like a person who is prepared to be accountable in their approach to the people you most respect and care about.

APPENDIX I

PERFORMANCE RECAP SHEET

S&W/Centerfoods Management Inc.

PERFORMANCE RECAP SHEET

Store Name:______________________________ **Effective Date:**__________

Name	Tech. Skills	Appear./ Clean	Punct./ Attend	Flex./ Avail.	Cust. Service	Sales Skills

Team Player	Speed/ Pressure	Upholds Standards	Total Score	Rank Order	Current Wage	New

5 = **Always** performs at a **High Level**

4 = Performs at a **High Level most of the time**

3 = Performs at an **Acceptable Level all of the time**

2 = Performs **below** an **Acceptable Level some of the time**

1 = **Fails** to perform at an **Acceptable Level**

PERFORMANCE RECAP SHEET DEFINITIONS

Technical Skills:
Performs all tasks in the station(s) they have been trained on, in a timely manner, with confidence, and with minimal mistakes. basis.

Appearance & Cleanliness:
Consistently conforms to all uniform guidelines, appearance standards, and hygiene practices.

Sales Skills:
Goes beyond customer service and employs suggestive selling techniques and offers samples on a consistent basis.

Team Player:
Consistently operates in a way that is beneficial to the entire team and the company. Is willing to step in and help when needed. Consistently possesses a positive attitude and promotes good will among all team members.

Punctuality & Attendance:
Is on time, in uniform, and ready to promotes good will among all team members. Begins work on time on a consistent basis. Rarely misses work, conforms to policy for calling if absent.

Flexibility & Availability:
Consistently works scheduled days, makes a minimal number of schedule requests, follows schedule request policy. Has some flexibility in days and times they are available to work.

Customer Service:
Consistently friendly and polite to all customers. Is able to maintain composure and positive customer service attitude when dealing with challenges or difficult customers. Possesses strong communication skills.

Speed & Work Under Pressure:
Consistently handles the pressure of heavy rush periods and is able to adjust to the increased production levels. Maintains positive attitude and willingness during busy periods.

Upholds Standards & Policies:
Consistently follows and supports all company policies, systems, and procedures.

APPENDIX 2

PERSONNEL ACTION FORM (PAF)

S&W/Centerfoods Management Inc.

PERSONNEL ACTION FORM

Check One:

☐ Termination

☐ Suspension

☐ Warning

Employee Name:____________________________________

Position:____

Store Name:_______________________________________

Date of Incident:____________________

Check One:

☐ Late

☐ Sick Call (with Short/No Notice)

☐ Uniform/Appearance

☐ Other (describe)___________________________________

____

____

Correction Action Required/Comments:

____

____

____

____

____

Employee Comments:

I have read and understand this document.

Employee Signature Date

Shift Leaders/Supervisor Date

Unit Manager Date

APPENDIX 3

FAIR TREATMENT/CONFLICT RESOLUTION FORM

S&W/Centerfoods Management Inc.

FAIR TREATMENT/CONFLICT RESOLUTION FORM

Date of Meeting:______________________

Attendees:____

____

____

Names of Aggrieved Parties:

A.____

B.____

C.____

D.____

Description of Incident or Conflict Which Required This Meeting:

____

____

____

____

____

____

____

A's Desired Result of This Meeting:

B's Desired Result of This Meeting:

Manager's Action Decision: (Deadlines set)

Signatures of All Attendees:

APPENDIX 4

WHAT MY DAD TAUGHT ME

WHAT MY DAD TAUGHT ME

1. Always tell the truth then you don't have to try to remember what you told somebody.
2. Cost more? Worth more!
3. If it was easy, anyone could do it! (and we wouldn't need you!)
4. If you have a conflict with someone, talk to them face to face. Don't go moaning to someone else.
5. You count the pennies, I'll count the dollars.
6. If you don't want to work harder, work smarter!
7. Things don't just happen. You make them happen!
8. Employees do not fail. Either we picked the wrong person or did a lousy job of training them!
9. What more do you need to know to decide? Act now!
10. Relationships are what are important! Dad never was concerned about a restaurant he owned and wanted to sell. It was just an inanimate thing. What was his biggest concern was the people who would be left there—whether they would be employed, whether he could bring them along with him.
11. Dad liked nice things but sacrificing financial security or relationships to have nice stuff was way off his radar. He was much more interested in making sure my mom felt secure and that his kids were taken care of than having a nice new car or jewelry.
12. Employees are not just "tools of the trade" or inputs. They are real, breathing humans who often have much more to teach you than you will teach them.

13. Dad often talked about a job for which he was recruited, working for a commercial laundry company. He got back from his route, and the owner of the company was at the warehouse as he was taking in his loads of dirty, filthy laundry. The owner said to him "I'm sure glad I've got you to do that job. I would never do it!" Dad got down off the truck, handed him the keys and told him "I don't have to do it either. Do it yourself!" and left the company. From that point on Dad rarely took the people who worked for and with him for granted. He was their equal, not their boss or overseer.

14. People, in general, want to do a good job. They even want to do a great job!

15. To lead people, you must have confidence in yourself, albeit with humility. People with poor self-esteem or self-image, "Low E" managers, often do not believe they really deserve the position they find themselves in. Their insecurities often result in management styles that are oppressive, do not create motivational atmospheres and/or are not great developers of people. In a few cases, the "Low E" managers are fearful of someone who is a subordinate taking their job. This fear can cause the Low E managers to not fully develop their staff or to do a poor job of delegating. The Low E manager often sees themselves as the only one who can do a job adequately, so they tend to hold tasks and jobs closely. This results in both overall poor management on their part and more turnover of the staff who desire to learn and grow.

ACKNOWLEDGMENTS

I would be remiss if I did not acknowledge the contributions of the many great people I worked with at S&W/Centerfoods. Managers, hourly employees, supervisors, and office staff all impacted on my learning and inspiration for this book.

Specifically, I want to recognize LeeAnn Halpin, Amanda Riley, Bret Stewart, Steve Bradshaw, Nathan Schauermann, Matt Wickham, Wayne Oxner, and Craig Schauermann. Their unique stories and willingness to share and be open made this endeavor a great joy.

My wife and partner, Barb Schauermann, has walked with me throughout this entire journey. Her patience, wisdom and insight have been invaluable.

KURT SCHAUERMANN

ABOUT THE AUTHOR

KURT SCHAUERMANN

Throughout his long career in the restaurant industry, Kurt Schauermann had to meet the constant challenges of sustaining a successful business while maintaining an enjoyable, balanced personal family life. His positive, caring attitude toward employees, colleagues, and restaurant guests, along with longstanding friendships beyond the workplace, proved to be so appreciated and impactful that he was encouraged to share his knowledge and experience in a book.

Drawing on articles, opinion pieces, memos to staff, and personal happenings, the author found *Lessons From The Front Lines* an inspirational journey to help young and older business owners find solutions to issues, no matter their cause, no matter their industry.

Kurt Schauermann and his wife Barbara live in a suburb of Seattle, Washington. He loves to play bridge, go on walks, and play golf (albeit poorly!) They have two adult married children and three grandchildren. Family time will always be the greatest joy for the two of them.